D0982694

More Tales from AGGIELAND

BRENT ZWERNEMAN

FOREWORD BY
DAT NGUYEN

www.SportsPublishingLLC.com

ISBN: 1-58261-969-7

© 2005 Brent Zwerneman

All photos courtesy of Texas A&M University.

All rights reserved. Except for use in a review, the reproduction or utilization of this work in any form or by any electronic, mechanical, or other means, now known or hereafter invented, including xerography, photocopying, and recording, and in any information storage and retrieval system, is forbidden without the written permission of the publisher.

Publishers: Peter L. Bannon and Joseph J. Bannon Sr.
Senior managing editor: Susan M. Moyer
Acquisitions editor: Mike Pearson
Developmental editor: Elisa Bock Laird
Art director: K. Jeffrey Higgerson
Dust jacket design: Joseph Brumleve
Interior layout: Kathryn R. Holleman
Imaging: Kathryn R. Holleman and Heidi Norsen
Photo editor: Erin Linden-Levy
Vice president of sales and marketing: Kevin King
Media and promotions managers: Kelley Brown (regional),
    Randy Fouts (national), Maurey Williamson (print)

Printed in the United States of America

Sports Publishing L.L.C.
804 North Neil Street
Champaign, IL 61820

Phone: 1-877-424-2665
Fax: 217-363-2073
www.SportsPublishingLLC.com

To the athletes of Texas A&M—without you these stories wouldn't exist, and I might still be writing about inverse floaters instead of reverse handoffs.

Contents

Foreword

There's no place like Kyle Field, and when I go back I still get goose bumps. I still get chills. There's nothing like running out onto that field, and the fans and students are just going nuts. You can feel the ground—even the entire stadium—shake when you make a play.

I've played in just about every stadium in the NFL, and there's nothing comparable to Kyle. To have experienced that is very special to me. Texas A&M is so unique, with our yell leaders and Sawing Varsity's Horns Off during "The Aggie War Hymn." When fans are swaying like that, opponents aren't even really thinking about the game—they're just amazed at the stadium. And it makes them dizzy.

But A&M is so much more than Kyle Field. If you're a student-athlete or a student—it doesn't matter. You're welcomed with open arms the first day you walk on campus and always greeted with the familiar and comforting, "Howdy!" It makes you feel at home.

That's one of the reasons you'll enjoy these stories from Aggieland—they'll make you feel at home again and make you laugh and maybe even wipe away a tear or two.

I've known Brent Zwerneman for more than a decade, back when I was a freshman linebacker at A&M in 1995 and he was just starting as a beat writer at *The Bryan-College Station Eagle*. He then "followed" me to Dallas as the Cowboys beat writer for the *San Antonio Express-News*.

I hung out with Brent after the Lombardi Award ceremony in Houston in 1998. We drank a beer together and toasted the trophy. He's always known when friendship is friendship and business is business, and I consider Brent a good friend and a true professional, and someone I've always trusted. I admire the way he carries himself and the way he does his job, and I've always enjoyed his colorful writing.

You will, too, in *More Tales from Aggieland*. I was fortunate to have attended Texas A&M when not only the football team excelled in the Big

12, but so did the volleyball, soccer, track, and baseball teams—it was almost like we all fed off of each other. Winning is contagious, and I'm so fortunate to have caught that fever at Texas A&M.

Enjoy the book and Gig 'em!

—DAT NGUYEN

Texas A&M's all-time leading tackler and standout Dallas Cowboy linebacker

Acknowledgments

Thank you especially to publisher Donnis Baggett and managing editor Kelly Brown of *The Bryan-College Station Eagle* for their graciousness in allowing material from *The Eagle* for use in this book. Thank you to editor Robert Rivard, managing editor Brent Thacker, sports editor Steve Quintana, and deputy sports editor Al Carter of the *San Antonio Express-News* for their unfailing understanding on this project and the use of some previously published material from the *Express-News* in this book.

Thank you to Dave South—the Voice of the Aggies—for his wonderful collection of memories and funny tales found in Chapter 9. Thank you to all of the sports reporters who contributed their sometimes funny and sometimes touching memories of covering the Aggies through the decades.

Thank you to the top-notch A&M sports information department folks for all of their help, particularly Alan Cannon, Chris Harrell, Brad Marquardt, and Debbie Darrah. Thank you to Elisa Bock Laird of Sports Publishing L.L.C. for her outstanding eye for editing.

And thank you to Steve French, Randal Matcek, John Pooler, David Ricks, and Tim Winn for their inspiration on this and other projects—and plots.

Introduction

My father, Willard "Bill" Zwerneman, grew up on a cotton farm near Dime Box, Texas, right between College Station and Austin, but an agricultural community more in line with the terra firma values of Texas A&M.

Funny how people have different memories of the A&M–Texas football rivalry—and some of those reminisces don't even include the games or stadiums. Like my father's.

His recollections of A&M–UT are gathering with friends and family on Thanksgiving Day on the front lawn of the farmhouse in the rolling, fertile hills of Dime Box and watching luxury cars in the 1940s and 1950s stream one way or the other on Old San Antonio Road—depending on where the game was that year.

Even as a child, he knew the A&M–UT game must be something special, because sometimes those cars were bumper to bumper in the middle of the country.

The rivalry lives on, and some of its more famous, infamous, or funnier moments are recounted in these pages, right along with loads of other tales collected through the years. I've had the pleasure of covering the Aggies for a decade, first for *The Bryan-College Station Eagle* and then for the *San Antonio Express-News*, and I'll value the friendships and wonderful people I've met in that span for a lifetime.

I was covering the NFL's Dallas Cowboys in 2001 when given the opportunity to return to Aggieland for the *Express-News*, and I jumped at the chance. As I said when I left *The Eagle* in 1999, Bryan–College Station is home to the finest, friendliest folks in the state, or at least the ones I've met.

More Tales from Aggieland recounts some of the stories of the athletes I've covered and stories encountered over the past decade, in what also was a golden era for A&M sports—based primarily on the football team's

1998 Big 12 championship and the baseball team's 1999 College World Series trip.

I also asked other sports reporters who've covered the Aggies over the decades to recount some of their favorite and vivid memories, and their eyewitness accounts are both humorous and tender. Like when reporter Olin Buchanan explains how Aggie running back Rodney Thomas placed coins into a broken vending machine after others had cleaned the snacks out.

Is there a better moment in summing up the A&M credo that "Aggies don't cheat, lie, or steal, nor tolerate those who do"—and who'd have thought a big, burly football player might be the model for such a lofty standard? Hope you enjoy these tales—I've had a blast covering the Aggies over the past 10 years, and look forward to continuing to do so.

SECTION I

On the Field

CHAPTER ONE

A Few of the Good Guys

Texas A&M prides itself on its friendliness, and so often that affability carries over to the field and courts. Here are a few tales of Aggie athletes who not only excelled in their respective sports, but also earned high marks for good manners, strong values, and respect for others.

No One Like Dat

Quang Pham said little in elementary school until Dat Nguyen entered his life. Quang, who was 11 years old in 1996—the same year Nguyen (pronounced "Win") was a sophomore linebacker for the Aggies—was about a year removed from his home of Vietnam. The youngster was still learning English at Mary Branch Elementary School in Bryan.

Nguyen met Quang through Aggie Athletes Involved, a community service organization, and the star linebacker—the first football player of Vietnamese descent at Texas A&M—spent about an hour each week helping Quang learn English.

Quang's fifth-grade teacher, Jennifer Paderas, knew Nguyen had made a difference in Quang's life when the youth came to class with his short black hair slicked back.

"Just like Dat," a beaming Quang said, pointing to his new hairdo.

"It can be hard for him to fit in with the American kids, because he doesn't speak English that well," Nguyen once said while helping Quang read a Beverly Cleary book. "The Vietnamese language is all singular, but he's really picked up on his reading."

For his part no one picked up the Wrecking Crew's way of doing things more than Nguyen, who wound up as the school's all-time leading tackler. Some of the greatest legacies Nguyen left behind in Aggieland weren't on the field.

No athlete in A&M history has probably left a more pronounced positive mark on the university than Nguyen, who went on to star for the NFL's Dallas Cowboys.

Former Aggie linebacker Chad Frantzen, a one-time walk-on, captured it best when he described how Nguyen befriended him. The two had a class together, and at that time Frantzen had no idea he'd one day suit up for A&M. Nguyen, a willing but not eager cover boy for college football magazines, eagerly chatted up his new buddy in class without a hint of pretension—never knowing he'd one day groom this fellow student for his position.

"He was an inspiration as much as any player I've seen," then-A&M coach R.C. Slocum said.

Bespectacled and a conservative dresser, Nguyen hardly looked the part of gridiron hero on campus.

"I'm not saying it was a split personality," Nguyen said, grinning, "but when you're away from football, you're away from football."

Considering he has become arguably the greatest football player ever at Texas A&M, it's hard to believe Nguyen once considered getting away from the sport in Aggieland. Slocum redshirted Nguyen, who weighed about 240 pounds at the beginning of his first school year in 1994.

After that Nguyen's heart felt nearly as heavy, and he almost headed home to Rockport for good a couple of times. Slocum described it as the disappointed player having the classic "Highway 6 look in his eyes" before he stuck it out in Aggieland.

The next year Nguyen became the first freshman to lead the Aggies in tackles.

Dat Nguyen made more tackles than any Aggie in history.

"The way he played is what the Wrecking Crew is all about," former A&M and NFL standout cornerback Ray Mickens said of Nguyen's style of play.

Because Nguyen stood only six foot one and possessed good but not blazing speed, many folks figured his football days might end in college. But even when Nguyen was still at A&M, Slocum said he figured there would be a place in the NFL for the best linebacker to ever don the Aggies' maroon and white. Why? Nguyen's heart was too big to be denied.

"He's one of those people," Slocum said then, "that you don't ever want to bet against."

DECEMBER 9, 1998
NGUYEN A WORTHY WINNER

HOUSTON – Call Dat Nguyen a hospitable Texan first, and toss in Lombardi Award winner somewhere in there for seasoning.

Nguyen, Texas A&M's star linebacker with a pipeliner's mentality (he's not afraid to get in the trenches), treated fellow Lombardi finalist and 370-pounder Aaron Gibson of Wisconsin to a Vietnamese meal on Tuesday, and then the Lombardi folks treated Nguyen to their award for the nation's best lineman.

"This isn't one of those cooked-up deals," a visibly excited Aggie coach R.C. Slocum said. "He did all of this on the field and played his way into becoming a nationally known player."

It's been a heckuva week to digest for Nguyen, who is also a finalist for the Butkus Award, which will be awarded on Friday in Orlando, Florida.

The keynote speaker for the 29th Annual Rotary Lombardi Award was former Dallas Cowboy quarterback Roger Staubach. Here's how the crowd of about 1,000 knew Nguyen won the prestigious award, announced by Staubach in the packed Hyatt Regency ballroom: "Gig 'em, Aggies."

The crowd erupted, whoops abounded, and Tina Turner's rousing anthem "The Best" kicked in over the loudspeakers. A standing ovation lasted a minute before Nguyen took the microphone.

"Goo—llly," he started—and he really seemed surprised by the magnitude of it all. "It's a shocker."

"That was just awesome," said Nguyen's girlfriend of two years (and future wife), A&M senior Becky Foster. "He's the most modest person, so I'm ecstatic because he really deserved it."

Tackles numbering 517 over the course of four years—by far the most by an Aggie and sixth among the old Southwest Conference, Big Eight, and new Big 12 Conference—will earn you such accolades.

So will giving new meaning to the term *Aggie ambassador*, as a graduate student who has constantly given back to his school and community over four years.

"We're extremely proud of him," A&M president Ray Bowen said. "He's a reflection of the values of his family, and he's brought to our university an enormous amount of talent. We couldn't be more proud of him."

When Nguyen stood at the podium, he mentioned with a wince how bright the lights were on stage. Sure enough, 30 minutes after autographing a truckload of programs, Nguyen looked much more comfortable surrounded by his girlfriend and five family members.

Nguyen grew up in the Gulf Coast shrimping town of Rockport, but he couldn't stand to fish. He didn't have the patience to sit around and wait for the critters to bite his line.

"He plays hard every week," Slocum said. "You say to yourself, 'How does he keep walking? He's got to be so banged up.' But the next week he's ready to go. He has one way of doing things, and that's full speed."

That's the way it's always been, said Nguyen's sister, Samantha.

"We didn't expect anything this big for Dat, but we know how hard he works," Samantha said. "He deserves it."

A surprise visitor to the proceedings was Texas running back Ricky Williams's mother, Sandy.

"I wanted to meet Dat, and I wanted to meet R.C.," Sandy said. "Dat and Ricky are friends, but Ricky couldn't make it because he has finals."

Slocum chatted about how Nguyen is a player truly appreciative of his scholarship and attending A&M,

evidenced by his already attending graduate school while playing his final season in Aggieland.

"I could go on all night about this young man," Slocum said.

He didn't, because Nugyen had an 8 a.m. flight to Florida.

It's a Snap

Kyle Lednicky didn't figure to earn much fame at Texas A&M playing his position in football. After all, it featured the same name as that of a sea-bottom dwelling creature.

But Lednicky, the team's deep snapper, recorded a pretty amazing statistic in his tenure at A&M (1995-1998): 538 snaps with nary an error. Not bad for a former All-District golfer from Houston's Stratford High.

Lednicky, who spurned the Ivy League to walk on at A&M as a third-generation Aggie, first learned to snap the ball in the sixth grade.

"I was one of the fattest kids on the team, so they put me at center," Lednicky said, grinning. "That was the beginning of my career."

And what a career. Lednicky snapped for the Aggies in 1998 when they won the Big 12 title game over Kansas State.

"This one will go down in history!" he yelled as he trotted off the field in St. Louis that December afternoon. So will Lednicky, for his extraordinary snapping skills.

> " I WAS ALREADY MAD, BUT HE HAD HIS OWN LITTLE WAYS OF TELLING ME I HAD SCREWED UP. "
>
> —Aggie deep snapper Kyle Lednicky after A&M associate athletic director Billy Pickard stopped in front of Lednicky on the sidelines and held his nose, waving his hand in front of it, after Lednicky snapped a couple of low balls in the 1998 Big 12 championship game

A Head on His Shoulders and a Hat to Go on It

Touted defensive lineman Ty Warren called together his family, friends, and the media to Bryan High School—a campus just a few miles north of Texas A&M—to announce his collegiate intentions that February 1999 day. Would he head west to Southern Cal, east to Tennessee, or south down 29th Street to College Station and A&M?

Warren had lined up a ball cap from each school on a table, and in a flair for the dramatic that might have made the Bryan theater arts teacher applaud and grin maniacally, Warren first reached for the USC lid before mumbling, "It's gonna be—A&M."

Warren's story of how he got to Texas A&M from East Bryan is pretty dramatic as well. He spent lots of time in the Bryan Boys & Girls Club while growing up and saw plenty of his friends veer onto a route other than one bound for Aggieland.

"Some of those people were more talented than me and should have been where I'm at," said Warren, who'd earned two Super Bowl rings with the NFL's New England Patriots by 2005. "But they chose a different road—drugs, dropping out of school, or just being lazy or whatever it is.

"I saw a lot of wasted potential, and I learned from the mistakes I saw other people make."

"MY WHOLE LIFE I WAS THINKING ABOUT GOING TO UT. BUT IT TOOK JUST ONE VISIT TO A&M TO CHANGE MY MIND."

—*Record-setting hurdler Larry Wade of Giddings,*
a two-time NCAA champion

Mama's Boy

Young Terrence Murphy learned to wipe the tears from his mother's eyes. During a string of heartaches in the Murphy family, six-year-old Terrence vowed he would never add to his mother's pain.

"He'd say, 'Mama, don't cry. I won't worry you like that,'" said Murphy's mother, Brenda Guthrie.

Murphy's older brother, former Baylor cornerback Kendrick Bell, later would spend time in prison for dealing narcotics. But no matter what they faced, Murphy remembered and kept his promise to stay on the straight and narrow for his mother's sake.

"I told her I'd never disappoint her," said Murphy, Texas A&M's all-time leading receiver who played from 2001 to 2004. "Growing up, I'd seen what other family members had done to my mom, and it hurt her a lot."

His clean living, combined with athleticism and a strong work ethic, resulted in Murphy's moving on to the NFL in the spring of 2005, as a second-round draft pick of the Green Bay Packers.

"That's why I've tried to work as hard as I can—for my mom," Murphy said. "I don't want her to have to work anymore."

Murphy believes it's the least he can do for the woman who never gave up on him, even though he was born more than six weeks early and because of bronchitis as an infant, barely could walk.

"I was a sick baby," said Murphy, who is six foot one and 195 pounds. "The first five or six years of my life, I was always in and out of the hospital. But my mama was always there for me. When I'd be awake all night because I was sick, she was in the room with me."

As a five-year-old, Murphy would hear people snickering at him. Why did that long-legged boy need to be carried around by his mommy?

"People always made jokes," he said. "She still carried me like an infant, even when I was that old. But her caring for me like that also gave us a very close bond."

In 2000, Murphy returned the favor. That's when his mother had emergency heart surgery and needed infant-like care.

"I wasn't supposed to survive, but the Lord saved me," Guthrie said. "Doctors said you don't survive what I went through—that I'm a walking miracle."

Terrence Murphy's love for his mother helped propel him to the NFL.

Murphy was still at Tyler's Chapel Hill High School then but managed to help care for his mother for a month at a hospital in Houston—and then for three months at a hospital in Tyler.

"He'd comb my hair and help dress me for church," Guthrie said. "Terrence took care of me."

Murphy could have declared early for the NFL draft and likely would have been selected in the first three rounds following his junior season. But he and his family took out a million-dollar life insurance policy in case of a career-ending injury, and Murphy returned for his senior year, based partly on his mother's admonition that he keep working toward his degree.

For his A&M career, Murphy finished with 172 receptions for 2,600 yards, both school records. Safety Jaxson Appel said when Murphy walked off the field for the last time for the Aggies, the program lost a great one.

"He's one of the few good guys left who plays this game," Appel said. "He's a devout Christian, and he is one of those people you really want to be associated with everything he does."

> "MOTHER WOULD USUALLY BRING YOU SOME COOKIES AND A $5 BILL BEFORE A GAME. IT MADE YOU FEEL BETTER."
>
> —R.C. Slocum reminiscing on the good ol' days and why recruits should play near their families

A Walk in the Park—or on the Court

Chris Walker was considered an ideal teammate in the spring of 2005, one primed to take his considerable skills to the highest level.

"He's a bright kid who interacts well with others," Hewlett-Packard manager Peggy Cruse said of her summer intern, who spent the summer of his junior year testing computer chips. "Chris will definitely have some opportunities out there."

The guys Walker played basketball with didn't think he was too bad, either.

"After what he's done," fellow starting forward Joseph Jones said of A&M's prized walk-on, "he ought to give a lot of people hope.

"[And] if you need to know anything about decimals or percentages or things like that, Chris has the answer like it's nothing."

Walker's hoops saga is at least as amazing as the idea that the Aggies' starting power forward also worked about 15 hours per week on computer chips.

"He's way too smart for me to even talk to," A&M coach Billy Gillispie said.

In the spring of 2004, Walker sat in Reed Arena among his fellow students for Gillispie's first press conference as the Aggies' new coach. Walker, who is six foot five and 210 pounds, had just won a championship at A&M. In intramurals. On a team dubbed "The Bill Waltons."

A friend seated next to him at Gillispie's press conference asked Walker if he might try out for the Aggies. Walker did, and he started the last 24 games as a non-scholarship player for the Aggies, who competed in their first postseason since 1994.

"I wanted someone who could catch the ball on the high post and reverse it, and Chris could do that," Gillispie said of why he started Walker.

Gillispie then paused, choking up a bit about the walk-on who meant so much to A&M's unforeseen success that season.

"There are other walk-on guys or whatever—but he's tough," Gillispie said. "I've never seen anything like what Chris has done."

Walker transferred to A&M in 2002 in search of a big-college atmosphere and a strong major after playing his freshman season at Division III UT–Dallas. He found both—and the bonus of playing Division I basketball.

During spring break of 2005, Walker arrived at Hewlett-Packard at 8 a.m. for nearly a full day of working on computers—before he went to basketball practice.

"It's amazing how everything has happened," Walker said during a hasty lunch break. "But the Lord has always blessed me when I've been faithful."

In turn, the muscular Walker faithfully provided the Aggies with a strong defender, good passer, and a role player who sank the occasional three-pointer. Asked if he dominated A&M's intramurals, Walker grinned.

"I kind of played the same role on those teams as I did with the Aggies," he said.

Then that blue-collar role may have occasionally caught the attention of the fellow pushing the broom in the rec center. In 2005 it roused the likes of Oklahoma coach Kelvin Sampson.

"I love that kid Chris Walker," Sampson said. "I just love his hustle."

Walker's physical and underdog style even earned the mockery of fans on the road in the Big 12, who chanted his name in places like Austin and Stillwater, Oklahoma. Walker considered that a badge of honor.

"It's pretty cool that they go out of their way to heckle you," he said. "I've got a lot of friends at those schools, and they said they were heckling me, too."

Walker was set to graduate in December 2005, and he wasn't certain whether he'd play his senior season. The big leagues of computers were beckoning, and job offers were flowing in.

"I'll always remember that I'm just a student—not anything special," Walker said of his mind-boggling season. "Just a student who got an opportunity to do what he loves."

"YOU ALWAYS SEE PEOPLE ON TV MAKING THE BIG PLAY, AND YOU NEVER KNOW HOW IT FEELS. NOW, I KNOW."

—Running back Sirr Parker after his touchdown defeated Kansas State 36-33 in the 1998 Big 12 title game

Small Time No More

Joseph Jones learned to play basketball on the grass in his backyard in Normangee, a rural community 30 minutes from College Station.

"Then the grass wore down to nothing but dirt," Jones said, grinning, "so we played on the dirt."

Jones, who is six foot nine and 240 pounds, played in a slightly different setting in his first Big 12 Conference game in the winter of 2005. Against No. 2 Kansas, a traditional powerhouse, the freshman Jones led the Aggies with 16 points and a game-high five offensive rebounds.

"Joseph Jones was the best player in the game," Kansas coach Bill Self said following his team's narrow 65-60 victory.

"I know that Joseph won't back down," Aggie coach Billy Gillispie said.

That's a trait Jones learned from his mother, Betty Jones, a single mom who raised five children. Joseph, who was recruited by rival Texas, signed with the Aggies in part so his dear mom, who worked in nearby Bryan, could attend his home games.

"I'm very honored, because there are not many kids who would consider their parents like that," Betty said. "Of course, that's the way I raised him to be. The good Lord and I did our best."

She also raised her youngest child to play basketball. Joseph was always the tallest kid in his class, even if he did graduate with only 46 other students from Normangee, whose biggest rivals are North Zulch and Snook. Jones's small-town roots, and his 1-A state championship earned in 2004, encouraged plenty of good-natured ribbing from his teammates.

"[Point guard] Acie Law talks about how he could have had a state championship if he had played Class A," Jones said, smiling. "But I've actually got one."

CHAPTER TWO

A Few of the Characters

Simply because Texas A&M appreciates conformity doesn't mean the personalities of the school have to be compressed—look no further than Stacy Sykora's Bozo doll that once dwelled in G. Rollie White Coliseum, right alongside Sykora's bemused and befuddled teammates. Here are a few Aggies who prefer the beat of their own drum under the auspices that it takes all kinds to make a team.

Hanging with Bozo

For four years around Texas A&M in the mid-1990s, you knew Bozo if you knew volleyball All-American Stacy Sykora, probably the most colorful athlete to ever dwell in Aggieland—literally.

"The same things that happened to Bozo," Sykora said of her longtime clown doll, "happened to me."

Bozo was Sykora's somewhat-disturbing—at least to those on the outside looking in—sidekick during her time at A&M, a little fellow who had been by her side since she was in the second grade.

Looking for examples to back up Sykora's cryptic quote? There are plenty. Bozo lost one of his big red shoes the night before Sykora competed in the state track meet when she attended Burleson High. Sykora lost her track shoe the next day.

Bozo later brandished a Band-Aid on his chin, and then Sykora's face broke out at the state volleyball tournament. Bozo, too, sported a Band-Aid on his noggin, which later in life began peeling from all of those years of protecting a make-believe cut.

"Bozo had brain surgery," Sykora explained.

The duo—and some more reserved individuals questioned this—don't have that in common.

Bozo was a regular on the Burleson bench during all of those competitive district matches, at least until the death threats started.

"When he started getting threatened," Sykora said with a face straighter than one her patented kills that brought her fame in College Station and beyond, "he started sitting up with my family."

Sykora, a raging beauty with a phenomenal vertical jump and a lion's heart, went on to play for Team USA in the 2000 and 2004 Olympics, but her star really began rising in College Station. And that's when she first started getting lots of attention for her quirky, yet endearing, ways.

Sykora's wardrobe screamed "Resale! Resale!" and her bedroom was a sensory overload that made unsuspecting visitors dizzy from—and here were just a few examples—love beads, a disco ball complete with spotlight, a "glowing hairball" (her description), Christmas lights, sprayed Woolite (it glows under the right light), flowery Sykora paintings, a jumbo portrait of a multihued Volkswagen "Magic Bus," assorted butterflies and frogs, incense, a glowing pink telephone, and a frightfully large poster of fellow eccentric Dennis Rodman.

Sykora loved to crank up the apartment stereo until her roommates' and visitors' ears practically glowed, like most of her room. Nearly lost in the crazy scene were all of Sykora's trophies and medals from her standout athletic career.

In the locker room at old G. Rollie White Coliseum, where Sykora delighted big crowds with her high-flying act, she plastered no less than five large pictures of Rodman in and around her locker. She also tacked a poster of Rodman peering from a bathtub above the locker room's shower door.

"I said that shows where the shower is," she said in justification.

Sykora realized that typically conservative A&M wasn't quite accustomed to tie-dyed everything, lifelike Bozo the Clowns, and an undying love for Rodman, but she said her time in Aggieland was priceless.

"The campus was so not me, but the school was so me," she said while wrapping up her illustrious career at A&M. "When recruits would come, I would show them my room, just in case they were a little different, too."

Sykora lived with a couple of other volleyball players while at A&M, including standout outside hitter Kristie Smedsrud.

"It was probably the most challenging thing I've ever been through, but also the most fun," Smedsrud said. "Sometimes we just sat around and watched Stacy."

"We could have charged admission and have people come in and watch her dance and do impressions of Lord knows who," roommate Jennifer Wells added.

Meanwhile, Bozo took in the whole scene from his perch in the Wonder Room, still armed with the emergency quarter—remember, this was before the widespread use of cell phones—stuck in his one red shoe that Sykora's mother gave her years ago.

"In Stacy's first year, Bozo was around quite a bit on road trips, but Bozo learned to stay at home," deadpanned Aggie coach Laurie Corbelli. "We thought Bozo was gross."

Sykora even carried a mug shot of her clown when the two were separated.

"There are a lot of people," Sykora explained, "who think I'm weird."

On the team's trip to Japan in the summer of 1997, the natives immediately labeled her *Aho*—the Japanese word for strange. But Corbelli said Sykora's teammates took to her free spirit.

"The team fed off of her, and she didn't even realize it," Corbelli said.

Sykora said her family was as normal as the next, and that her grandmothers—MaMaw and NaNa—possessed exceptional senses of humors.

"Sometimes I sit around and wonder what happened to me," Sykora said with a big grin. "I've always been the clown in the family."

Bozo begs to differ.

Stacy Sykora's teammates drew the line at Bozo sitting on the team bench during games.

"IN AUSTIN, THERE'S A LOT MORE TO DO THAN IN COLLEGE STATION. YOU'VE GOT SO MANY WEIRDOS DOWN THERE THAT YOU HAVE TO TAKE CARE OF THEM WITH A VARIETY OF CLUBS. DOWN HERE IN COLLEGE STATION, EVERYONE'S PRETTY NORMAL SO EVERYONE ENJOYS THE SAME CLUBS. WE CAN HANG OUT TOGETHER.

"BUT DOWN THERE, THEY HAVE TO HAVE ABOUT 18 DIFFERENT SETTINGS FOR 18 DIFFERENT BREEDS OF PEOPLE. THERE ARE PEOPLE WITH EARRINGS ALL OVER THEIR FACE AND BODY, LIBERALS, TREEHUGGERS, AND GRANOLA GIRLS."

—Aggie center Steve McKinney,
who went on to a solid NFL career

Not Skirting the Issue

One of Texas A&M's all-time toughest football players wore a skirt when he chilled out. Hey, easy now, former offensive lineman Semisi

Heimuli, the Aggies' first player of Tongan descent, said there was lots to love about "lava lavas."

"You can relax and kick back in them," Heimuli said of the skirts, which Tongans wear. "I think they're more comfortable than shorts."

Nobody at A&M messed with Heimuli, even when he was wearing his colorful skirt. The six-foot-one, 300-pound tough guy wound up starting a record 51 games. Two of his cousins, Moses Vakahali and Lee Foliaki, later played for A&M.

Heimuli said he started the "Tongan tradition at A&M" when former Aggie defensive line coach Bill Johnson, a spirited sort, visited his home in Euless, Texas, and immediately challenged him to a wrestling match.

"If I beat you, you're going to come to A&M," Johnson declared to the startled high school recruit.

The showdown never actually hit the mat, but Heimuli liked Johnson's fervor so much he signed with A&M.

A&M's Jumping Jack of All Trades

The scene: Texas A&M's 10-meter high dive at the student recreation center in the summer of 1999.

The characters: A frightened few Aggie football players huddled at the top. And one brave soul completely in his element.

"Everyone was daring each other to jump off of it," A&M offensive lineman Chris Valletta said. "The next thing we know, Shane Lechler runs to the very back of the platform and waves at us."

Valletta then recalled Lechler's graceful plunge as eloquent as any scene from *The Nutcracker.*

"Shane gets a running start and launches off the side as far as he can, and he just lays out in a full swan dive and cuts right into the water, not even making a splash," said Valletta, shaking his head at the memory. "The other guys just lowered themselves off the edge."

Aw, shucks, it was nothing, said Lechler, who didn't exactly use that choice of words but recognized a decent anecdote and dutifully added a touch of color.

"That's all from coming from a small town," said Lechler, an All-America punter at A&M from 1996 to 1999 and an All-Pro with the Oakland Raiders. "We'd swim in the rice canals every day in the summer, so that was no big deal."

Shane Lechler's remarkable ability to punt just scratched the surface of his athleticism.

Reminded the rice canals around East Bernard usually aren't equipped with 10-meter high dives, Lechler nodded.

"Yeah, I know, but why be scared?" he said. "It's just water."

Lechler once frowned when asked, "If you were to attend a convention for punters and kickers, whom would you hang out with?"

"If it was all punters and kickers, I might be by myself," he said. "People say I'm not your average kicker. I kind of hope I'm not. Occasionally, you'll run across one that's pretty normal—a guy who likes to hunt and fish and who doesn't mind having a good time every once in a while—but not very often. Kickers and punters are just really wiry. They're little people."

Lechler is six foot two and 240 pounds, and he finished his career as the all-time NCAA punting leader with an average kick of 44.7 yards.

"Shane Lechler is one of the greatest players who ever played at Texas A&M," Aggie coach R.C. Slocum said.

Lechler pretty much served as the program's Babe Didrikson Zaharias—a multifaceted athlete—of the late 1990s.

"I've never seen an athlete as good as Shane," Valletta said. "He can throw a pinpoint pass 70 yards downfield and then go out on the golf course and shoot a 70 [actually in the high 70s], and he'll light you up on the basketball court."

Valletta conjured images of Olympic diver Greg Louganis with his description of Lechler's rec center plunge and then summed up Lechler's career in five words: "What can't the guy do?"

Flash and Dash

There hasn't been a funnier, wittier player who's sashayed through College Station in recent memory than Dante Hall, the flashy running back, receiver, and return man who went on to a superstar career in the NFL with the Kansas City Chiefs.

Hall arrived at A&M in the fall of 1996 from Houston's Nimitz High and immediately chose the No. 34, which Leeland McElroy had worn before him. McElroy, who'd finished his career the year before, was one of the NCAA's all-time most prolific return men.

"At first my teammates called me 'Little Leeland' and 'Fake Leeland' and all of that," Hall said. "But that became my number."

Early on in his career in Aggieland, Hall described his dream business he planned to open after his playing days were done.

"I want a car wash that's got a beauty salon attached that cuts men's and women's hair," he said. "It won't be some little shimmy-sham or hole in the wall. You'll get your hair done while the car is getting washed or your toes are getting done—the whole nine yards. Whatever your body needs."

Hall also embraced his reputation as a social butterfly around Bryan–College Station.

"I just like to have fun—I hate to be bored," he said. "I need some excitement, I can't be around dull people. I just tried to spark up conversations with the girls at the clubs and interact with people."

One time his interaction with his fellow Aggies got him in trouble during a game. In a September 1997 game at Kyle Field against Southwestern Louisiana, Hall "raised the roof" right next to the Corps of Cadets after getting knocked out of bounds. The Corps went wild. The act earned Hall a 15-yard penalty for unsportsmanlike conduct.

"If Dante's act was wrong, then we need to change the rules," coach R.C. Slocum said at the time. "We can't have a bunch of robots out there. When you've got all of your fans right there, what are you supposed to do, frown?"

In his four seasons at A&M, Hall left plenty of opponents frowning with his ability to bob, weave, and slash on the field. He finished as one of the Aggies' all-time leaders in all-purpose yards, although he left the team during his senior season because of a dispute with Slocum.

Hall holds the A&M record for punt return yards in a season with 573, set in 1996. He quickly proved himself as an outstanding punt returner, and Slocum once humorously described the manner in which the coaches pegged potential returners, by lining up all of the freshmen running backs, receivers, and defensive backs and yelling, "Catch this!"

"A lot of them are like, 'Boom!'" Slocum said during an animated demonstration of the sound a ball makes careening off a shoulder pad.

"You can either catch them or you can't," Slocum said. "The first day Dante walked out there, he was a natural at catching the ball."

And quickly catching on as one of Aggieland's all-time most colorful athletes.

"ZIG, ZIG, ZIG, ZIG, ZAG."

—Aggie running back Dante Hall describing one of his moves

Dante Hall, who once said he hoped to open a beauty salon, provides a complimentary facial to a defender.

Following the Road

Texas A&M tight end Boone Stutz wasn't named for a small town in Oklahoma. He was named for a road sign pointing toward a small town in Oklahoma.

"I was adopted, and when my parents came to pick me up [in Fort Worth] from Shawnee, Oklahoma, they saw a road sign that said, 'Boone, Oklahoma,'" said Stutz, the Aggies' resident country boy and the team's featured tight end during the 2004 season.

Not bad for a wide-grinning young man—one who might have been named "Stillwater" or "Norman" had his parents chosen a different route home to Shawnee—who traveled quite a back road leading to Aggieland.

Stutz, a junior in 2004 who also served as the Aggies' long snapper, originally played for A&M coach Dennis Franchione at Alabama before Franchione bolted from Tuscaloosa, Alabama, in December 2002 for College Station. Stutz had originally wanted to play for Franchione at TCU, where Franchione was before going to Alabama in December 2000.

"Boone is a great story, from where he started in high school to where he is today," said Franchione, who awarded Stutz a scholarship in the spring of 2004. "Every young athlete could draw inspiration from the Boone Stutz story."

Stutz didn't even start in high school but said that he loved football too much to give up on it. It didn't hurt that he's six foot five and came out of high school weighing about 295 pounds. By the time he was wrapping up his A&M career he was at about 260. Or 261, if you counted the red-strapped fishing glasses he constantly wore around his neck.

"I feel naked without 'em," said Stutz, who also liked to wear a bright green baseball cap that proclaimed, "Truckin' for Jesus!" stuffed over his shock of red hair.

"I could imagine Boone with his own fisherman's show [on TV] someday," Aggie offensive lineman Aldo De La Garza said.

Wanna Fight?

Aldo De La Garza's opponents learned to be aware—very aware—of the intimidating six-foot-four, 320-pound offensive guard. He earned his black belt in jujitsu while attending A&M. He said he applied what he learned in martial arts to the football field.

"It's like a six-second battle out there on the football field," De La Garza said. "When you're one on one with a guy in jujitsu, that [battle] can roll over to football, too. I feel like I kind of have the edge in football, because a lot of people just don't know how to fight."

CHAPTER THREE

Inspirational Aggies

I f Rich Coady had settled for the scouting report on his abilities coming out of high school, he'd never have won a Super Bowl ring with the St. Louis Rams—or even played safety at A&M. The Aggies below will tell you that many things worth gaining in life don't come easy and that often their faith lifts them through rugged times.

Trial Through Fire

The fire tried swallowing Rick Rigsby, but the flames only fed his faith and spirit.

Rigsby, an ordained minister, is a senior lecturer in the communications department at Texas A&M who also served as the football team's life skills coordinator. He also is an ordained minister.

The players also watched as Rigsby dealt with a tremendous grief in his life. In September 1996 Rigsby's wife of 18 years, Trina, died of cancer.

"My sermons are born out of my experiences, and so lately I've been speaking on the values of going through the fire," Rigsby said at the time.

"That there are blessings that you might not imagine are obtained as you walk through the valley of death.

"I've been challenging men to cherish their wives, because you just don't know. You just don't know."

For four months following the death of Trina, his college sweetheart, Rigsby cried and couldn't stop.

"Finally, I had to make a choice," he said. "I just had to hold onto the hand of the Lord, knowing that the tough times couldn't last forever. The thing that helped me was the realization that I had to look beyond my own grief. That I had two little guys who were looking at Daddy every single day, and I could either dwell in my own grief or say, 'Boys, sometimes life isn't fair, but you can't stop.'"

The Brazos Christian School, where Trina was a librarian, now houses the Trina L. Rigsby Memorial Library. The A&M football team watched Rigsby suffer through his first wife's death, but stay strong in his faith throughout.

"I don't understand why she died at age 41," Rigsby said. "But I don't need to understand that. That's God's business."

His unwavering beliefs left an impression on the Aggies.

"It's hard to put into words how highly I think of him," kicker Kyle Bryant said. "He's impacted my life a lot. I'm encouraged and impressed by him standing steadfast in his beliefs, with what he's been through. That kind of strength rubs off on everybody. He's a unique example of what every man should try and be like."

Rigsby offered these encouraging words to those who have their own struggles:

"There are good things that can come out of difficult times," he said. "A real genuineness, a real humility, a real passion for the things in life. In many ways, I feel like the most blessed man. How can that be when I had just gone through hell?

"My central message to people is that we live in a society that loves to receive, and we don't know how to let go. We have celebrations of grabbing onto and holding onto—marriage, anniversaries. But a large part of life is learning to let go, and you can survive."

Rigsby added that simple life is key.

"The reality is I'm a simple guy," he said. "I just have a basic life, and I just want to make a difference in someone's life."

On the first Father's Day following Trina's death, Rigsby said that after church he and his two sons, Jeremiah and Andrew, planned to "go

A&M professor Rick Rigsby provides Aggie football players with an example of unflappable faith through his deeds.

find a pond and drop our fishing lines in the water"—which also served as a gentle reminder of Psalm 23 from the Bible: "The Lord is my shepherd; I shall not want. He maketh me to lie down in green pastures; he leadeth me beside the still waters. He restoreth my soul."

But Rigsby's story of love didn't end there. Two years after Trina's death, he met the lovely Janet Butcher at a morning Bible study. The two were married soon thereafter.

"I like to say our love was born out of the heart of God," Rigsby said. "God didn't just take care of me, he took care of my entire family. To those who are hurting, I'm living proof miracles can happen."

Maybe the most important message from Rigsby, a man who seems to have all of the answers, is that he doesn't have all of the answers.

"You still struggle," he said. "But it's okay to struggle. It's okay if things don't always fit, and it's all right if you don't always have all of the answers. But I've been given the peace to just rest in God's perfect will."

"EVERY AGGIE WILL CRAWL OUT OF EVERY CAVERN AND CAVITY IN THE NORTH AMERICAN CONTINENT, AND THEY'LL BE RANTING AND RAVING AND SCREAMING DOWN THERE IN THAT STADIUM, AND THERE WILL BE ELECTRICITY FLOWING. AND THERE WILL BE MARCHING BANDS ... AND GOOSESTEPPING AND ALL OF THAT STUFF. IT'S GOING TO BE TEXAS A&M FOOTBALL."

—*North Texas coach Matt Simon before the Aggies stepped all over the Mean Green 55-0 in 1996 at Kyle Field*

Walkin' on

No one knew better than former Texas A&M safety Rich Coady the stigma of "walk-on" tagged to your name.

"Nobody even gave Rich a chance when he came here," former Aggie tight end Dan Campbell said. "When you met him it was like, 'Hi, I'm Rich Coady, walk-on,' and you just kind of dismissed him. And then he just came out of nowhere on the field and started making plays, and you couldn't believe this kid didn't get a scholarship."

Coady, however, early in his career swept the label "walk-on" somewhere beneath the mats of the Netum Steed weight room. The poster boy for what a walk-on could become at A&M later became more apt.

"If what I did helped a high school kid come and work hard and contribute—if he knows that it can be done—then that's great," Coady said.

Coady earned a scholarship as a sophomore in 1996, along with a starting job in the Aggies' secondary. Coady's father, Richard Coady, played for the NFL's Chicago Bears from 1967 to 1975, but that still didn't help his son earn a college scholarship out of Richardson's Pearce High.

Not even the University of North Texas, practically in Coady's backyard, offered him money to play football. His name may not have been spelled right on his first A&M jersey—"Cody"—but Coady wound up a three-year starter at strong safety for the Aggies.

"He was one of those I called a *program guy*," former Aggie coach R.C. Slocum said. "He did everything you asked. He was a hungry football player. We didn't have to "de-recruit" him. A lot of guys come in and they've been told all of this stuff in recruiting, and then they think they're getting screwed because they didn't play their first year.

"But a guy like Rich came in with his feet on the ground and said, 'Tell me what I have to do.' They're hungry and they sometimes end up surpassing some of the stars that may have had a little more talent."

Coady even turned the unglamorous number of 48 to something of a memorable one in his inspiring span at Texas A&M.

"Don't think that I chose that number," he said, grinning. "Another thing about being a walk-on is you're the last to get your number. It was between 48 and 49. I just said give me one of them. I'm happy to have one of them."

Coady, at six foot one and 200 pounds, wasn't some *Rudy* type of player who was all heart—he was also plenty of muscle and fitness. By the time Coady was an upperclassmen he regularly finished among the team's top performers in offseason strength and conditioning. He also cut out caffeine and carbonated drinks and avoided fat foods to become the best football player he could.

"That way you kind of felt like you were doing everything you could to be a good football player," he said. "I don't ever want to look back and say, 'I wish I would have lifted more, ran more, or ate better.'"

His plan worked. Coady parlayed his exceptional work ethic into a long NFL career—and he even earned a Super Bowl ring with the St. Louis Rams in 1999.

Coady offered simple advice to youngsters who want to chase their dream—even as a walk-on.

"It's really hard to overcome being a walk-on to your coaches," Coady said. "You're not a guy they watched a lot in high school, and recruited scholarship players are expected to play, and coaches push them to play. My best advice is to just be prepared, because you never really know when you're going to get your chance."

DECEMBER 6, 1998
SENIORS STEWART, PARKER COME THROUGH WHEN IT COUNTS

ST. LOUIS – Extra consonants their mamas gave 'em aren't the only things Branndon Stewart and Sirr Parker share. Not after they'll be linked in Aggie glory following Texas A&M's extraordinary 36-33 victory over second-ranked Kansas State on Saturday in the Big 12 championship game in the Trans World Dome.

Not after both seemed to have glided into the sunset and been replaced by guys named Randy (with one "R") McCown and Dante (with one "N") Hall. No doubt people still patted the backs of Stewart and Parker, mainly because they're good people who had wound up solid role players after entering Texas A&M with huge fan expectations.

Stewart, the heralded transfer from Tennessee; Parker the stud running back from California. Those things happen, right, when players don't really pan out? Stewart made a nice backup, and Parker occasionally flashed that speed the coaches raved about, but little more. They were nothing to get worked up about—on or off the field.

Aggies are good people, so it wasn't like fans were calling for their heads for not meeting great expectations. They just didn't call for 'em. Now you can go ahead and add some exclamation marks to their already odd monikers, because Branndon! and Sirr! chose a grand finale for finishing up at A&M.

Stewart, who started in place of an injured McCown, completed 15 of 31 passes against mighty K-State and for the most part looked like he'd been bedazzlin' back there the entire season.

"We had no doubt whatsoever Branndon Stewart wouldn't miss a beat," KSU coach Bill Snyder said.

As for Parker, he burned K-State for the game's final touchdown, on a 32-yard catch and run that showcased his, guess what, blazing speed. Call it the lighter side of divine intervention, since the bygones Stewart and Parker were key reasons A&M won the best game Aggie fans ever saw.

"It's unbelievable the way they stepped up," A&M tight end Dan Campbell said. "But, you know, they've both been there before."

Right. It was déjà vu, all over again, as Stewart and Parker were huge in A&M's overtime victory against Oklahoma State that propelled them to the Big 12 South Zone championship in 1997.

"On a football team, everyone can't start, and a lot of times guys who aren't starting cause a lot of problems and become concerned with their own interests," A&M coach R.C. Slocum said. "It's very fitting that the two stars of the game ended up being two young men who had demonstrated all year very unselfish attitudes."

Stewart said on Saturday that he was lucky to attend A&M, because even when his playing days are done he'll always be a Texas Aggie. Parker joked that he was happy to be a guy who's not only a football player, but one who played one on TV.

"You always see the people on TV making the big plays, and you never know how it feels," Parker said with a grin. "Now I know. You've got to keep your ego in check in this game. Every player in college football thinks he should be playing more than he's playing. If you're not playing and you're losing, that's one thing. But you can't ask the coaches to change it if it's not broke.

"I guess it's all about opportunity."

Do you believe Texas A&M won its biggest game since the Aggies won the Sugar Bowl—now their likely destination—following the 1939 season to win the national championship? It's hard to imagine a bigger victory—although Slocum says all games are relative to the time they're played—but certainly you can't name one better for its drama, and for A&M fans, its outcome.

"Wooo, weee," one Trans World Dome employee said.

"That's the best game in this building since it was built."

The tales within this game were as unbelievable as the outcome, starting with Stewart and Parker. Both are good guys and good stories—ones with great endings at Texas A&M.

His Sister's Keeper

Robin Van Zant grew to expect the soft taps on her bedroom door and the "You all right?" from roommate and younger brother, Tim, in the still of night. They were queries as regular as the alarm clock that awakened her for class several hours later at Texas A&M.

"He was always checking up on me," said Robin, diagnosed with juvenile diabetes at the age of 13. "It made me a lot less anxious with him always making sure I was all right, because I knew that if there had been an emergency, Tim would be there."

Robin then paused, and added with a smile about her brother, a receiver for the Aggies from 2001 to 2003: "I don't know, maybe my mom made him do it."

Folks back home in Victoria, Texas, and friends in College Station knew Robin was kidding, because there might not be two tighter siblings than Robin and Tim Van Zant.

"We're probably closer than any brother and sister I've seen," Tim said. "We're more like best friends."

Robin later attended graduate school at the University of Houston, but she and Tim lived together for two and a half years in Aggieland, where she was an undergraduate. And any potential suitors of Robin always had to pass the Tim Test.

"Everyone was kind of reluctant," Robin said, grinning, "when they found out my brother played football."

Tim, a standout football and baseball player at Victoria High, took a circuitous route in earning a scholarship to play football for A&M. In fact, Tim had played a couple of years for free until the end of the 2003 two-a-days, when first-year coach Dennis Franchione approached him, hand outstretched.

"Congratulations, I'm putting you on scholarship," Franchione told a grateful Van Zant. "You've earned it."

Robin knew that as well as anyone. She remembered the many days Tim showed up at their College Station apartment, worn and bruised from another day's practice as a walk-on.

"It was hard on him, because he had walked on to this huge team, and he was the low guy on the totem pole," she said. "But he never complained about it. He just said he was going to stick with it."

Tim stuck with it to the tune of earning the 2003 Aggie Heart Award, the highest honor for a Texas A&M senior football player. That season, he finished second on the team with 30 catches for 367 yards, and he also returned 14 punts for 75 yards.

Not bad for the Victorian who spent a good part of his college life looking out for his big sister and much of the rest trying to earn a scholarship to play some football for the Aggies.

"You work and work and you hear all of these other guys talking about their scholarship checks," Tim said. "Sooner or later you start wondering if it's all worth it. I found out it was."

The Soldier on the Gridiron

The blood oozing down Josh Amstutz's leg gave it away.

Otherwise, amid the howl of gunfire in a suburb outside of Baghdad, Iraq, he wouldn't have immediately known that a sniper had just shot him that April morning in 2003.

"Your adrenaline is flowing so much at that point, you don't even realize it," Amstutz recalled. "But then I saw the blood. I thought, 'This could be a quick two minutes.' You bleed out real fast if a bullet hits an artery."

A year later, Amstutz only thought of a two-minute warning in football terms. A Purple Heart veteran whose route to college included an appearance on a TV game-show bonanza and a tour of duty in Iraq, Amstutz was a walk-on safety at Texas A&M in the fall of 2004, a support role consisting essentially of practice-team duty.

The year prior he was serving as a corporal in the Marines, part of the invading force that stormed into Iraq in the spring of 2003. His value to the Aggies, teammates say, stretches far beyond his contributions on the practice field.

"Josh is my hero," A&M guard Aldo De La Garza said. "Here we've got a guy on our team who took a bullet for our country to help protect our freedoms."

"It's very admirable what he's done for his country," safety Jaxson Appel said. "And now he's getting to live out another one of his dreams."

Because of a luckless bullet, Amstutz got that chance.

"I had a lot of prayers from family and friends on my way over to Iraq," Amstutz said. "I felt those prayers when I was there—they provided a shield around me. Even when I got shot, I knew it was all going to work out the way God wanted it to."

The bullet avoided an artery, and it didn't hit bone. Amstutz recalled a feeling of calm after he was wounded, even though the sniper was still hiding among the buildings of that Baghdad neighborhood. Amstutz said he realized he still had a job to do.

"It was starting to hurt, but I was so concerned with getting my stuff to the other Marines, that I didn't really think about it," he said.

"It crosses your mind that this could be it, but you've got to keep going. If you start screaming and acting scared, everyone else is going to be like, 'Whoa, what's going on?' If you keep calm people might think, 'He got hit, but he's going to be fine.' Even if I wasn't going to be."

Amstutz's fellow Marines loaded him into an armored vehicle, and he was airlifted to a hospital. Within a day, he was able to call his wife, Jessica. She already had received a call from the Marines. Her husband had been shot, she was told, but he was going to be okay.

"Are you going to able to walk?" Jessica asked her husband. "You can tell me the truth."

He reassured her that he would, indeed, be able to walk. A year later, he was running up and down the practice fields at A&M.

Amstutz, who grew up on a farm in Indiana, met Jessica—now a teacher in Bryan—at a church singles group in Alexandria, Virginia, in early 2001. An A&M graduate, she was working for Fox News in Washington.

He was a member of the Presidential Honor Guard at the time. In January 2001, Amstutz was part of the detail that escorted George W. Bush from Capitol Hill to the White House after his inauguration.

That fall, after they became engaged, she took him to the A&M–Texas football game at Kyle Field. Sitting in the stands at Kyle and inspired by the school's spirit, Amstutz decided he wanted to try to play football for the Aggies—once he had fulfilled his duties as a Marine.

Before that happened, however, Amstutz had a couple of scenes left to play out in his *Forrest Gump* script. The first took him to Hollywood. The second to Baghdad.

Before he left for Iraq, Amstutz attended a filming of *The Price Is Right* with his wife and parents. Dressed in Marine blues, he was picked from the audience as a contestant and won a furniture grand prize in the show's "Showcase Showdown."

He left for Iraq before the show aired. Jessica showed him the video—and the fancy new furniture—when he returned.

"It was cool," Amstutz said with a grin.

But not quite as cool, he said, as suiting up for the A&M football team. He dressed out for the first time in the fall of 2004 when the Aggies played Oklahoma at Kyle Field. He suited up again in the Aggies' victory over Texas Tech the following week. His assigned number is 39.

"A lot of people came up to me and said, 'That's a good number—that's the last year A&M won a national championship,'" Amstutz said. "It was amazing to run out on to Kyle Field, running through the Corps of Cadets, and everybody's yelling and screaming—just amazing."

But one thing football is not, he is quick to assure, is war—despite the popular analogies between the two. Two years ago, Amstutz was like many others—watching the news and considering Bush's warnings that war in Iraq was imminent. When it finally happened, and Amstutz was dispatched to help fight it, his focus on the task narrowed considerably.

"It goes from this big international war to simply protecting your buddy," he said. "It goes from thinking, 'What's the world going to think of this?' to 'This guy is in the fighting hole with me. This is who I'm protecting. This is who I'm fighting for. And he's doing the same for me.'"

And to Amstutz, that kind of huddle was what mattered most.

CHAPTER FOUR

You Can't Beat Baseball at Olsen

O lsen Field has been home to Texas A&M baseball since 1978 and is considered one of the nation's best venues for college baseball. Here are a few tales from Olsen's clubhouse and beyond, many centered around Texas A&M's last College World Series team in 1999.

A Mother's Love

Does the Lord work in mysterious and sometimes funny ways? Judy Scheschuk thinks so. So went the recruitment of her youngest son, John, by then-Texas A&M baseball coach Mark Johnson in the mid-1990s.

While wooing John Scheschuk, a standout first baseman at Pasadena's Dobie High, Johnson discovered an amazing sight in the form of an old scrapbook photo. It showed a schoolboy Johnson in a New Mexico All-Tournament Baseball Team uniform with Jim Scheschuk, a genetic carbon copy of the boy he was recruiting.

"It was unbelievable," Johnson said, grinning. "That picture may have helped a little bit in recruiting."

Scheschuk, one of the most affable and bright-eyed athletes ever to grace Aggieland, went on to star at A&M and served as the team captain of the Aggies' 1999 College World Series team.

"John had natural ability when he was two years old," his mother said. "He would spiral the football when throwing with Jim. We thought that was something."

Those early years would be the only catch Scheschuk played with his dad. Jim Scheschuk died suddenly from a blood clot when John was barely three, and his mother, at 34, was a widow raising three kids.

"You don't think about it, you just do it," Judy Scheschuk said. "It was the hand I was dealt, and I made being their mom and dad my priority. God gave me these kids to raise, and I had to do the best job I could."

Scheschuk—along with his sister, Debbie, and brother, Mike—is a testament to his mother's success.

"What a personality!" Johnson said of his team's leader in the late 1990s. "He was one of the guys who yelled, 'One heartbeat!' and it just had so much meaning. And when you talked to Judy, you just couldn't help but feel good. She had that twinkle, and John had that."

Jim and Judy met on a blind date while freshmen at the University of Texas. Jim was an All-Southwest Conference catcher at Texas, but the Vietnam War cut short a professional career in the Los Angeles Dodgers organization, when he enlisted in the Marine Corps. In the A&M media guide, Scheschuk listed Jim Scheschuk as his favorite pro athlete.

Soon after his father's death in 1980, Scheschuk watched a baseball game on TV.

"Mommy, I want to do that," he said, pointing to the pitcher.

So Judy took Scheschuk outside and tried to teach him a wind-up. One problem: she was right-handed and he was left-handed.

"I would have won a video contest if we'd have been on tape," Judy said of that comical first lesson.

Scheschuk grew into a strapping first baseman who was later selected in the seventh round of the Major League Baseball draft by the San Diego Padres. And Judy, a church secretary, was there every step of the way— with scorebook in hand.

Scheschuk, who always turned to his mother for advice, said he dealt with not having a father as best as possible.

"There were two ways to look at it," he said. "You could pout your whole life, or just go on with it. Some guys' dads left their families by choice, and to me that's a much more difficult deal."

> "I KNOW HOMETOWN KIDS ARE SUPPOSED TO GO TO THE HOME-TOWN COLLEGE AND ALL OF THAT, BUT I WANTED TO GET OUT OF WACO. IT SEEMED LIKE EVERYTHING BAD HAPPENED THERE SINCE [MY FAMILY] MOVED THERE. THE BRANCH DAVIDIANS AND ALL OF THAT STUFF."
>
> —Aggie pitcher and big-leaguer Casey Fossum,
> on why he signed with A&M over Baylor

Nicknames

Steve Scarborough grimaced when that girl in high school nicknamed him "Screech" after the shaggy-haired, scrawny fellow on the TV show *Saved by the Bell*.

"Hey, 'ppreciate it," Scarborough thought. "That guy is pretty ugly."

When Scarborough arrived at Texas A&M as a shortstop in 1996, his teammates found out about the nickname. And it stuck. No sport is better for nicknames than baseball, particularly college baseball—even the ones that transcend prom and carry on to the fields of higher learning.

"Even Coach [Mark] Johnson started calling me 'Screech' when I was a freshman, because we had like 14 Steves on the team," Scarborough said.

Johnson had no idea who the original "Screech"—or for that matter, what *Saved by the Bell*—was.

"Apparently he looked like somebody," Johnson said, grinning.

In baseball, it's even somewhat disdained to be called by the name parents anointed their children. One time, former Aggie catcher Shawn Schumacher tried formally introducing one of the team's assistant coaches, Jason "Hutch" Hutchins, to a friend. The untidy transaction went something like this:

"This is, uh, um, Hutch ... um, Hutchins ..." Schumacher had no idea what the man's true first name was. Johnson got a little nostalgic when discussing the tradition of nicknames in college baseball.

"In the past, coaches had a nickname for every player," Johnson said. "I've heard some coaches try to give some guys a nickname to try and make them feel like a certain type of player, like 'Speedy' or something. Now, when I was recruiting [former infielder] Sittichoke Huckuntod, for example, well, you just can't even get in a comfortable conversation when you sit there and say, 'So, Sittichoke, what do you think about this or that? And I really didn't want to call him 'Choke,' but that's what it came down to."

Sometimes the nicknames can be even more brutal. Early in his A&M career, former pitcher Khalid Ballouli was known as "K.B." around the locker room. But then for a stretch Ballouli had trouble striking out some batters, and so because he was short on Ks, his teammates unmercifully cut the "K" from his nickname and just started calling him "B."

But while creativity is at a premium with nicknames in college baseball, players often still fall back on the old standby of "Sally" should a ball scoot through a player's legs or something of that ilk.

"Or we just call them by their girlfriends' names," former Aggie infielder Sean Heaney said.

Scarborough had an explanation as to why nicknames are so prevalent in baseball and not so much in other sports.

"Some of it has to do with the history of baseball, which is very well known," he said. "And then there are a lot of left-handers in baseball, and left-handers are the weirdest people alive. They're usually the people who come up with all of this stuff."

Aggie left-hander Shane King was known for throwing his dipped snuff on players in the shower and getting away with it because he claimed it was good luck. So, what do his teammates call a guy with a name already fit for royalty?

"Usually just a cuss word," King said, grinning.

Superstitions

Texas A&M's 1999 baseball team, the school's last squad to advance to the College World Series, served as a case study in the art of superstitions in baseball.

"Baseball is cruel because you don't play good games all of the time," said Mark Johnson, who coached the Aggies from 1985 to 2005. "You play so many games in a season that if you play a good game, you say, 'Geez, what did I do?' So, the next day, you say I'm going to go out and do the same thing.

"I like people thinking about winning and doing whatever they can to win, and superstitions kind of fall in that category, because you're thinking about a formula for winning."

Former Aggie shortstop Steve Scarborough's formula for winning included wearing the same hat all of the 1999 season—a putrid jewel that turned dark pink as the season wore on because it bled so much maroon.

"It was old, dirty, smelly and the stitching was coming off," Scarborough said. "Really, it just stank. Every day when I put it on, I had to get used to the smell all over again."

The 1999 team listened to the tune "Tops Drop" before every game, which was provided on CD by third baseman Dell Lindsey. Most of the players didn't particularly care for the song, but no one would have dared suggesting changing the routine, because they had whipped an opponent earlier in the season after listening to it for the first time, and it became a part of their formula for success.

Center fielder Steven Truitt attributed part of his success that season to a youngster who gave him a Starburst candy every time he was on deck to hit. As of 2005, no A&M baseball team had revisited the College World Series. So any future Aggie squad may want to borrow a few of the superstitions from that last CWS team.

> "JEFF WEIBLE WAS OUR CATCHER AND HE'S A BIG GUY. HE'S LIKE 240 POUNDS, AND THE FANS LOWERED A TWINKIE DOWN ON A STRING FROM THE SECOND DECK, RIGHT INTO OUR DUGOUT. SO WEIBLE ATE IT, OF COURSE, BECAUSE HE NEVER PASSED UP A MEAL IN HIS LIFE."
>
> —*Washington baseball coach Ken Knutson on the first time his team played at Olsen Field in 1993*

Rabbit Ears

First baseman John Scheschuk was known as one of the finest, most personable gentlemen to ever play for the Aggies. But even gentlemen have their lapses.

A&M visited Sam Houston State's Holleman Field one dreary April 1997 afternoon, and Scheschuk was out with an injury but still in the visitor's dugout. After a particularly poor call by the umpire, Scheschuk piped up, "You're terrible, rabbit ears!"

The not-so-endearing term *rabbit ears* is usually directed at a player or umpire who pays a little too much attention to some razzing. Sure enough, this umpire was paying attention.

"Hey, Mark," the umpire yelled toward Mark Johnson, "No. 24 is out of here!"

Scheschuk, who'd never been tossed from any game of any kind from Little League on, lowered his head and headed for the team bus. Later, he divulged there had been a little more to the story: When he called the umpire "rabbit ears," he'd also lifted two fungo bats at angles off of the top of his head, simulating, you guessed it, rabbit ears.

Chicken Strip

Texas A&M fans became familiar with feisty freshman left-hander Jason Meyer during the 2004 season, when he earned freshman All-America honors for an 8-2 record and 2.89 ERA. What they didn't know is Meyer owns an awfully strange appetite. You might consider him a meat-and-potatoes kind of guy. Minus the potatoes—and definitely hold the gravy.

"Makes me gag," Meyer said, crinkling his nose, when asked if he even eats cheese.

Meyer's diet was so one-sided—typically consisting of chicken or a plain hamburger—that his Aggie teammates affectionately dubbed him "Chicken Strip." Meyer's parents used to try to make him eat vegetables.

"They told me I couldn't leave the table until I ate 'em," Meyer said. "So I would just sleep at the table. They finally gave that up around the sixth grade."

Meyer, five foot 10 and 175 pounds, may not have won any nutritional awards, but he won a bushel of games early in his A&M career by feeding batters a steady diet of fastballs, curves, and change-ups.

> "THEIR FANS RODE US REALLY HARD, BUT AFTER THE GAME WE HAD PEOPLE INVITING US OUT FOR BARBECUE. IT WAS KIND OF A UNIQUE EXPERIENCE."
>
> —*Aaron Sele, big-leaguer and former Washington State pitcher, on pitching against the Aggies at Olsen Field*

APRIL 19, 1997

ROWDY OLSEN FANS CLAIM IT'S ALL PART OF THE GAME

Observations from the second deck of a record crowd of 7,255 at Olsen Field on a beautiful Friday night:

"I will cut off all the horns of the wicked." —From a Psalms Bible verse and printed on T-shirts worn with a burnt orange longhorn, sure enough, with its horns chopped off. Only in this rivalry between Texas A&M and Texas could the Bible be twisted to make one of the schools look bad.

I'm sitting in the squeezed-shouldered section just beyond the rails, and the seats have long since been snatched. It's still 45 minutes until game time, and the ragging has started.

Your first impression—before you observe them for nine innings—of the gang of the few that lines the rails and screams at the opponent is this: Goofs, get a life, you've got too much time on your hands, the last time you played ball was in Little League when the other kids made fun of you.

But once I took it all in, well, my impression didn't change a bit. But that was okay, they were having fun and gave the crowd something to laugh at.

The night in the crowd starts with a rush of adrenaline and much forearm bashing and chest-bumping among the raggers. They've got so much juice early their screams—complete with ever-reddening heads—are often indecipherable and often leave the crowd scratching its collective head.

This was new Texas coach Augie Garrido's debut at Olsen as Longhorn coach, and he was greeted with "We want Gus" cheers, the crowd sarcastically wanting one last shot at former UT coach Cliff Gustafson. Garrido probably preferred that one to "Soggy Burrito," which came later in the game.

You get the feeling these guys are frustrated stand-up comedians, who hold the crowd—which is there to see a baseball game—captive. Or maybe a better word is hostage.

If you ignore them, they won't go away. They'll only get louder. Three times, security visited the raggers to tell them to quit climbing on the rails. One pointed out that if they didn't want 'em a'climbin' up there, they ought to put a sign up.

Some of these guys are the antithesis to the sentiment, "A good sense of humor is an offspring of intelligence." While they're for the most part funny and quick-witted, you get the idea some aren't the brightest lamp in the living room.

These guys certainly contribute to A&M's home-field advantage, but they're a little bit like the crazy great aunt other family members try and ignore. Here's a tip to any psychology professor on the A&M campus: Take your class to a ballgame and let them watch an extremely interesting case of human behavior.

Portly Texas pitcher Chris Speerstra took the mound in the first inning to chants of "Free Willy!" and "Did you eat Bevo before the game?" Soon following was, "Pitcher's got a big butt!"

Those drew laughter, of course, much of it of the nervous variety from parents who brought their kids to a ballgame. But to the Raggies' credit, the ragging never jumped past PG-13.

One of the game's lighter moments came when a Lite beer truck tooted "The Aggie War Hymn" on its trek down Wellborn Road. The crowd erupted in delight. When a train cruised the tracks outside the outfield, the fans begged the Aggie batter to "hit the train."

It's hard to imagine anything like that in Austin.

In the top of the sixth, the umpire bent over to dust the plate. "Pitch it now!" the crowd yelled.

By the bottom of the sixth inning and with the Aggies nursing what would become the final score of 6-3, either from pure exhaustion or from the buzz wearing off, the rail-huggers were almost polite. About that time, an exuberant, round Texas fan simply called "Wilson" who had loaded up on barbecue and beer, did a little jig to "Joy to the World" (not the Christmas version) to the fans' joy.

That's when the "Wilson is drunk!" chant started, and the fans had switched their attention from the field to each other. The gang's quick-witted ringleader, a former student named Jimmy Harrison, says the ragging is all in fun.

"It's baseball, and it's part of the game," Harrison said. "It goes back to Little League, when kids would make fun of each other."

Harrison considers his stand-up routine directed at the opponent, which admittedly is pretty funny, as a vent and a stress-reliever. He says the group knows where to draw the line, which is at using profanity.

"But we're heavy on innuendo," he said with a grin. Harrison says many of the fans come to the game to "see a big group of idiots on the front row making fools of themselves."

I'm not sure how the gang affects attendance, but I won't argue with the latter. But it's all in good fun, right?

CHAPTER FIVE

Just for Grins

I f Aggies possess at least two things, they are loyalty and a sense of humor. In good times and in bad, Texas A&M athletes and coaches have managed to sometimes grin and bear it. Here are a few of those stories.

Infernal Accusation

A scary situation turned downright ghoulish at the Southwest Conference Track & Field Championships in May 1996 in Lubbock. Texas A&M junior Kari Wyatt was running the 10,000 meters about as well as she ever had, heading into the final 100 meters.

"Barring a total collapse, she'll finish fourth or fifth!" an ecstatic A&M coach Greg Hinze told an observer during the race.

That's when the 100-degree heat at R.P. Fuller Stadium on the Texas Tech campus set in, and Wyatt totally collapsed.

"I just hit a wall," Wyatt said. "I got mentally and physically tired and started weaving, and my eyes rolled back."

At that point, longtime A&M trainer Mike "Radar" Ricke sprinted onto the track and started to grab Wyatt.

"She was saying, 'No! No! Get away, Radar!' But I'm used to that, because that's what my wife and daughter tell me all of the time," a grinning Ricke said.

Wyatt, still delirious minutes after being pulled from the race, was upset she wasn't able to finish. A&M trainer Patty Berthot tried to calm Wyatt by telling her she'd done a fine job.

"But you don't understand," Wyatt told Berthot, "Coach Hinze will take away my meal money. He's the devil!"

A day later a fully recovered Wyatt said she had simply felt bad about what she considered letting Hinze down.

"He would never ask us to do anything that he didn't think we could, and I felt like I should have finished that race."

Hinze, who later went on to a successful stint as Sam Houston State's head track coach, never confirmed or denied Wyatt's infernal accusation.

"No comment," he said with a wicked smile. "I thought that was one of the all-time great quotes. It was really funny, even if it what happened to Kari wasn't funny at the time. I'd like to think she meant it in an affectionate way."

Wild Tale

In Troup, Texas, the folks are friendly and the squirrels are scrambling. Ask former A&M receiver and Florida native Albert Connell, who once tasted a little Deep East Texas cuisine courtesy of Troup native Eddie Jasper, an A&M defensive lineman from 1994 to 1996.

"Albert was over at my house, and he sat down and started eating," said Jasper, who went on to a long career in the NFL, primarily with the Atlanta Falcons. "He didn't even ask what it was. So when he did, I told him it was polecat."

It turned out Jasper was joking, as Connell began spitting out the culinary oddity.

"It was really wild hog," Jasper said, laughing, "and that made him just about as sick."

Dat Can't Hit the Curve

Dat Nguyen, one of Texas A&M's most decorated athletes and one its all-time nicest guys, did have one flaw that his cousin, Chau Ngo, consistently exploited. Nguyen, the greatest linebacker to ever play at A&M

who carried on his talents to the Dallas Cowboys, couldn't hit an electronic curveball.

"I beat him in [video] baseball," Ngo said. "But I can't beat him in football, period. He knows all of the defenses I'm going to play before I play them. But I kill him in baseball. I throw him curves and change-ups, and he can't touch those. He's too impatient for the breaking balls."

That impatience, so helpful as a linebacker who's supposed to doggedly sniff out the ball, carried over to the favorite pastime of Nguyen's hometown, the coastal enclave of Rockport. Nguyen never could stand fishing, because it required sitting around and waiting for a fish to bite.

No wonder Nguyen finished as the school's all-time leading tackler with 517.

Chicken Chat

Tony Barone, A&M's beleaguered basketball coach from 1991 to 1998, tried a little bit of everything to entice fans to G. Rollie White Coliseum. In the fall of 1997, Barone even took his pitch to the legendary Dixie Chicken in the Northgate bar district.

He gave a "Chalk Talk" to beer-guzzlin' masses that night in the Chicken, which probably explained the increase in overall-clad customers at the Aggies next home game.

> "IF THEY DON'T COME, I'LL JUST TAKE THE HOT DOGS HOME."
>
> —Tony Barone, after he bought lunch
> for 500 before a game

Sidelined by *Sidelines*

Most folks at Texas A&M figured the biggest risk in allowing ESPN cameras all-access to the 2001 football team for a reality show called *Sidelines* was simply a bad season.

Hyper coach Tony Barone often shed his clothes—to a point—to make his points on the Aggie sideline.

"They said it was going to be like a soap opera," Aggie linebacker Christian Rodriguez said. "And I was like, 'How can you make a soap opera out of football?'"

He figured it out quickly.

The mostly conservative A&M faithful probably never figured the footage gathered outside Kyle Field would cause the most couch-squirming. They probably never thought they would see scenes of two women kissing outside a Bryan bar, and a main character whose outfit was an orange jumpsuit with "psychiatric ward" emblazoned on the back.

"I've spent a lifetime trying to project an image of what Texas A&M is all about," a concerned Aggie coach R.C. Slocum said then. "And I wouldn't want it to be distorted on a national sports show—or what was billed as a sports show—that shows us as something we're not."

The A&M football media guide pitched *Sidelines* as a "docudrama told through the eyes and voices of those directly involved with the team and through those in the community who are affected by Aggie football."

The first episode drew mostly good reviews from Aggies, because it centered on a successful effort by students to blanket Kyle Field in red, white, and blue for a game in salute to the tragedies of September 11, 2001.

The second episode briefly featured quarterback Mark Farris and also a number of bar scenes showing two apparently drunk coeds hanging out with a male student who wasn't a member of the A&M football team. The young man drove the women home in the show, but not before the two ladies kissed for the camera.

"If you ever saw an advertisement for not drinking and driving," the program's executive producer Rick DiGregorio said in defense of the scene, "it was that show."

Farris and his wife, Neocia, let their six-year-old daughter, Kameryn, only watch certain parts of the episode.

"As soon as we saw the drinking and the going out to the bars and all of that stuff, we took her out of the room," Farris said. "As a football play-er, I'd rather have seen more about football."

ESPN chose A&M for its first season of *Sidelines* over the likes of Notre Dame and Michigan. By season's end, the show hadn't won Slocum over.

"I was in New York for a few days, and the comments I got were all good," Slocum said at the end of the year. "But you don't know if people were just making conversation or that they really watched the show. They would say, 'It's good,' and I would say, 'Really? Which show did you watch?'"

> "I SIT DOWN, AND I'M GETTING READY TO TALK, AND I START SMELLING SOMETHING THAT DOESN'T QUITE SMELL RIGHT. AND I LOOK DOWN, AND I'VE GOT THIS BIG OL' GOB OF DOG POOP ON MY SHOE. SO I STARTED LOOKING AROUND TO SEE IF I HAD TRACKED ON THE FLOOR."
>
> —*R.C. Slocum on his memorable recruiting visit to Chris Cole's home in Orange, Texas. Cole signed with the Aggies anyway.*

Sibling Rivalry

Jason Glenn usually got his way growing up near Humble, Texas. When he didn't, his mother said, his back stiffened and he fell flat on the floor as a semi-act of rebellion. But his older brother, Aaron, finally cured him of that curious habit.

"Aaron whooped him," Rosie Glenn said with a chuckle. "He broke that up. Jason didn't get stiff anymore."

Aaron and Jason Glenn were separated by seven years, but each made their mark playing football in Aggieland.

Aaron played cornerback in the early 1990s; Jason played linebacker in the late 1990s. Each earned All-Conference honors, and each went on to a solid career in the NFL.

Jason was the 10th of Amos and Rosie Glenn's 11 children. He recalled some sprints home between he and Aaron from the barbershop in Humble, and the brotherly competition they fostered.

"Aaron would always say, 'Do you want to race me?'" Jason said, grinning. "I would take off, and he would always catch me by about the fifth step. He'd get right beside me, laughing, then I'd try to grab his shirt, and he'd just run away and leave me. He'd be home for 10 minutes when I finally got in."

Jason idolized Aaron and remembered Aaron's first year—1992—at A&M out of Navarro Junior College in Corsicana, Texas.

"He told me he was going to be starting for the Aggies, and I was like, yeah, whatever," Jason said. "Then I saw him play against Stanford in the Pigskin Classic on TV, and I said, 'Hey, that's Aaron.' He made his first tackle, and he jumped up, and the family went crazy. Ever since that day, I dreamed about seeing my family jump up from watching me on TV."

Despite Aaron starring at A&M, Jason briefly considered signing with rival Texas in his recruitment out of Aldine's Nimitz High.

"He said he wanted to go to Texas because Aaron went to A&M," Rosie said of Jason's abrupt rebellion.

But Aaron had a simple and to-the-point message for his little brother: "We can't have that in this family."

Aaron once scored nine touchdowns in a game in the local Little League back home in Little League, so Jason then set his eyes on that prize.

"In one game I had scored six touchdowns by halftime, and the whole crowd was yelling things like, 'You've only got three more to tie and four more to break it!' In the last quarter, I had nine touchdowns and was running with the ball all alone when I tripped over my feet, right at the 10-yard line. I never had a chance to score after that."

Jason smiled. He wouldn't have changed a thing.

Brotherly Love

Seth McKinney can at least say he was warned when older brother Steve shot him in the foot with an arrow.

"We were shooting arrows at a beach ball, and I went up there in front of him to get my arrows, and he had told me not to," Seth said. "So he ended up shooting his, and it went in my foot. I was shocked."

Steve, then 11, didn't mean to stick his eight-year-old brother, just scare him a bit.

"I aimed low," Steve said, laughing a bit at the memory. "I wasn't even trying to hit him. But when I did, you'd have thought I nearly killed him. He ran screaming and crying to the babysitter. I tried bribing him with money, and even told him I'd give him my Nintendo if he wouldn't tell our parents."

Seth told, all right.

"I'm sure I did," Seth said. "I can remember the babysitter picking me up and holding me."

That'd be a mighty tough task these days. Seth joined his older brother Steve in the NFL in 2002 after each enjoyed a standout career on the offensive line at Texas A&M.

And these days the agile Seth doesn't have nearly as much trouble with his feet as he did as a kid. For its part in the turmoil, the arrow only caused an abrasion. But during Seth's senior year at Austin Westlake High School and immediately before his first football game as a senior, he tripped while performing a "hat dance" during a pep rally on the gym floor and broke a bone in his foot.

"I guess I just got a little carried away," said Seth, who wound up earning his master's degree from A&M. "I missed the first five games of my senior year."

And despite the little things in life such as wayward arrows, Steve and Seth served as the other's best man in their respective weddings.

"That's how brothers are," Seth said, smiling. "That kind of stuff happened all of the time, but we're true friends."

"IT'S KIND OF LIKE WATCHING YOUR DOG GET HIT BY A CAR."

—Texas A&M offensive lineman Cameron Spikes's description of what it's like to allow a sack of the quarterback you're trying to protect

---

Blair and the Longhair

Texas A&M women's basketball coach Gary Blair might have figured he needed to tack a "no shoes, no shirt, no service" on the front door of his home, in his first season in Aggieland in 2003-2004.

Such a sign might have come in handy after the ever-genial Blair offered four free tickets to an Aggie game on a Bryan–College Station radio show—then gave out his home address for pickup. Five minutes after the on-air tender, Blair's doorbell rang.

"The young man had no shoes, long hair, the whole nine yards," Blair said, chuckling. "He looked like he'd wandered off of the pig trail back in Arkansas."

Blair, then in his first season of trying to revive A&M's stuck-in-the-mud program, couldn't have been happier to see the fellow, who eagerly claimed two tickets, one for himself, the other for his girlfriend. And in a stark reminder that Blair, a renowned coach in women's basketball—had lots of work to do at A&M—no one claimed the other two.

"WHEN PEOPLE TALK ABOUT THE PRIDE OF AGGIELAND, THEY'RE LEGITIMATE. I'LL BRAG ABOUT LIVING HERE UNTIL THEY PUT ME IN A GRAVE. WE LIVED AND DIED WITH EVERY SINGLE BOUNCE OF THE BALL. UNFORTUNATELY, WE DIED WITH IT."

—*Eddie Molitor, an assistant basketball coach under Tony Barone*

The Jiggler

Oklahoma forward Kevin Bookout lined up for a free throw in the winter of 2005 at Texas A&M's Reed Arena—and grimaced. The Jiggler had claimed yet another victim in the sometimes not-so-friendly confines of the Aggies' home court.

"That dude was huge," said Bookout of shirtless A&M fan Nathaniel Cooper, who tipped the scales at a gravity-challenged 310 pounds. "He started shaking and I went, 'Ugh!' He was just going nuts."

Cooper, who at least offered the formality of a bow tie with his eye-catching ensemble, typically lined up behind the opponent's basket and quivered, shivered, and gyrated during free throws—effectively shaking his moneymakers. His efforts earned him such nicknames as The Jiggler, Jiggly Puff, Fat Shaker, and the Fightin' Texas Aggie Belly Dancer.

"People tell me all of the time they love what I'm doing," Cooper said.

Well, most, anyway. Cooper said one A&M fan kindly asked that he please, please re-robe.

"He was an Old Ag who graduated in like 1945," Cooper said.

One Internet poster on texags.com even wittily dubbed Cooper's act as "one big wardrobe malfunction"—a reference to the Janet Jackson bare breast incident in 2004 during the Super Bowl halftime show in Houston.

The A&M basketball team, however, presented to Cooper, then a senior sociology major, a pair of Aggie shorts and shoes for his, um, services. A&M officials said they briefly discussed asking Cooper to keep his shirt on, but then reasoned that fans show up with painted bare chests and such all of the time at a variety of sporting events.

"Some people are ashamed of their bodies," Cooper said. "But I figure that God gave me this body and this personality, so I'd go out and have fun with it."

And that attitude even earned the admiration of Bookout, a standout player for the Sooners.

"That's courageous, for him to take his shirt off like that," Bookout said. "I'm a big boy, too, and I wouldn't have the courage to do that in front of all of those people."

"THERE WAS A BIG FRUIT BASKET [IN MY HOTEL ROOM], AND IT WAS SIGNED FROM REVEILLE. WHEN I WAS IN THE SOUTHWEST CONFERENCE, I WAS NEVER TREATED ANY BETTER THAN WHEN I CAME HERE."

—*Oklahoma State coach Eddie Sutton,*
who coached at Arkansas earlier in his career,
during a visit to College Station

Billy Ball

In his first basketball season at Texas A&M in 2004-2005, coach Billy Gillispie typically ran his team during practices until his players' tongues dragged. But on the day after a 14-point defeat at Texas Tech in 2005, he made the frustrated Aggies' feet drag instead.

"He made us walk through the whole practice," A&M guard Antoine Wright said. "He told us, 'If we're going to walk in games, then we're going to walk in practice.' He even made us stop talking."

That season the Aggies were welcomed to Gillispie's unorthodox and occasionally funny world, one in which the A&M coach sometimes bristled at suggestions he owned some unconventional means of doing things. Whatever he did in his first year at A&M, it worked. The Aggies earned their first postseason bid (to the National Invitation Tournament) since 1994 in only Gillispie's first season.

"Everybody in the conference needs to understand that A&M will not be an easy place to play in the future," Oklahoma State assistant coach Sean Sutton said.

The Aggies typically hustled through a full-scale practice even on game day.

"This team needed to learn how to practice," said Gillispie, who guided Texas–El Paso to the NCAA tournament in 2004, in only his second season with the Miners. "We weren't going to waste a game day to not get better."

Gillispie said he didn't care if his team was picked to finish near the bottom of the heap in the Big 12—as per custom since the Big 12's inception in 1996.

"So if you're supposed to finish 12th in the Big 12, does that mean you're not supposed to practice hard? I don't believe in that," Gillispie said. "Every team across the country that's trying to win a championship, I promise you, is practicing extremely hard."

Wright said he talked with a few of his peers in the Big 12 about the Aggies' game-day practices. He said his sounding boards included Oklahoma's Taj Gray and Missouri's Marcus Watkins, who transferred from A&M in 2004 following the dismissal of his father, Melvin Watkins, as the Aggies' coach.

"No team does what we do before a game," Wright said. "Those guys think I'm making it up when I tell them about it—they don't believe me.

They say, 'You're just trying to make him seem like a harder coach than he really is.'"

It was also like pulling teeth to get Gillispie out of a pressure man defense for a game's 40 minutes, even if his opponents had less success in prior contests against a zone.

"If they catch the ball three feet farther out, then they have a harder time throwing it to the post," Gillispie said. "Plus, the shooters in this league are too good. I don't like guys getting open looks."

A couple of times in his first season Gillispie left practice in disgust—only to secretly watch from a room above Reed Arena.

With the 45-year-old Gillispie, a Graford, Texas, native who cut his teeth in the Texas high school coaching ranks, one of the few predictable things one got in his first season was the oft-repeated mantra that his team will "play hard, play smart, and play together."

And that was enough for his players, who appeared to have bought wholeheartedly into their coach's occasionally unorthodox way of doing things.

> "I NEED ALL YOUR PRAYERS. BUT MORE IMPORTANTLY YOU NEED THE PRACTICE."
>
> —Tony Barone to reporters
> after he was reassigned as A&M basketball coach

Taking Coach Too Seriously

Only Shelby Metcalf could have spun a yarn about a white mule at a black-tie affair. When the former Aggie basketball coach was inducted into the Texas A&M Hall of Fame in November 1998, Metcalf told a wild tale that involved him and Barry Davis, who played for the Aggies from 1975 to 1976.

The two went hunting, and by request of the owner of the property Metcalf was to shoot the guy's old white mule, who had served the family well but whose time had come. So Metcalf played a joke on Davis and told him that the property owner was an angry fan—and to get revenge Metcalf was going to shoot his mule.

"But before I could tell him it was a joke, Barry had shot two of the guy's calves," Metcalf said, grinning.

Ricky and Dat

In the days before his first game against Texas A&M in 1995, Texas freshman running back Ricky Williams, dreadlocks pouring out the top of a UT tennis cap, took time from a cup of fruit salad to give a thumbs up.

"They go like this or something," Williams, a San Diego, California, native said of A&M's hand sign. "Gig 'em. What is an Aggie anyway? Is it an animal? I saw a little sign that said, 'I brake for all animals but Aggies.' So I thought it was an animal."

Sensing a shy, good-natured goofiness that would become a Williams trademark over his time in Austin, his teammates gave him an especially hard time as a freshman.

"A lot of our defensive players like to make fun of me," Williams said then. "Before we played Texas Tech, they said, 'Watch out for [linebacker] Zach Thomas! He's going to get you!'"

His fellow Longhorns also warned Williams, who wound up winning the Heisman Trophy award in 1998, about A&M's Wrecking Crew defense, then led by fellow freshman sensation linebacker Dat Nguyen.

"They told me to watch out for the whole defense," Williams said in the days before his first game against A&M. "They told me it's the No. 1 defense in the country, and you're not going to get your 101 yards. We'll see."

Williams wound up rushing for 163 yards in UT's 16-6 victory to claim the final Southwest Conference championship—and something else happened along the way.

He began to form a friendship with Nguyen, and by the time they were playing their final game against each other in 1998, Nguyen had given Williams one of his A&M helmets, and it hung on Williams's wall in his apartment in Austin.

"I'm sure when he tackles me," Williams said with a grin before their final college meeting, "we're going to have a few nice words for each other."

Witty coach Shelby Metcalf made his team wear leisure suits while traveling in the 1970s.

The two continued their friendship on into the NFL, where Nguyen's career actually outlasted that of the more heralded Williams.

Nice Tries

People do the darnedest things to try to get into a Texas A&M–Texas football game after the tickets have long since been sold. Just ask A&M sports information director Alan Cannon, who's served in that capacity since 1989.

One of the more creative ways in recent memory came when a George Lucas-wannabe requested media credentials from Cannon.

"The gentleman said that he had written a screenplay about the A&M–Texas game and that he would like to sell it to Hollywood, and he wanted to bring a director with him," Cannon said.

Right. The old, "I'm writing a screenplay and my roommate will direct bit." After checking into the request, Cannon couldn't find any verification that the guy was legitimate. So he denied the request. It was a nice try, though, and maybe that fellow's creativity will pay off on the big screen.

Another man once used the sentimental approach to try to tug at Cannon's heartstrings.

"He said the only thing his grandson wanted for Christmas was to watch the A&M–Texas game from the sidelines," Cannon said. "I had to explain that the sidelines are a working area for people like photographers, not to mention one of the worst places to watch a game."

NOVEMBER 27, 1997
FAT BURGER AND OTHER TALES OF A&M AND TEXAS

When they're not stuffing down cheese fries and hot wings, offensive linemen say the darndest things. Especially before a Texas A&M–Texas clash on the football field.

So what makes an Aggie an Aggie and a Longhorn a teasip? (Hey, I know my target audience).

"If you're a Longhorn, you hate the Aggies," explains Texas offensive lineman Ryan Fiebiger. "And if you're an Aggie, you hate the Longhorns."

Fiebiger—A&M's Yell Leaders dubbed him "Fat Burger" at Bonfire—reminisced about when he and teammate Brent Kelly road-tripped to College Station and pulled over on this or that side of Caldwell and peeled Kelly's Longhorns stickers off of his truck.

"He was afraid his tires were going to get slashed," Fiebiger said.

While Fiebiger feared the rivalry might provoke some auto damage, Aggie offensive lineman Steve McKinney lived it.

"Whatever!" McKinney barked when relayed Fiebiger's sad story of mistrust. "What's he talking about? I went to the mall in Austin and somebody keyed all around my A&M sticker. They're the ones who are hostile."

When they're not partying, anyway. The Texas guys always trot out Sixth Street as an example of why Austin is a better, livelier town than College Station.

"To me, there are so many more things to do in Austin," Fiebiger said. "I mean, you have Sixth Street."

McKinney and Fiebiger finally agreed on something.

"In Austin there is a lot more to do," McKinney said.

"You've got so many weirdos down there that you have to take care of all of them with a variety of clubs. Down here, everybody's pretty normal, so everyone enjoys the same clubs. We can hang out together, but down there, they have to have about 18 different settings for about 18 different breeds of people.

"There are people with earrings all over their body, liberals, treehuggers, granola girls ..."

And apparently, that's only four breeds of 18.

Texas's Phil Dawson and A&M's Kyle Bryant are two of the best kickers in the nation and even better guys, so Dawson chose his words carefully when comparing the collegiate settings.

"Austin is a city," he said after some thought, "and College Station is not. I would say College Station is probably more of a college town. I guess you wouldn't call Austin a college town because there's a lot more going on. Next question."

The booters agree, too.

"College Station is smaller than Austin, but you can feel the camaraderie and unity better here," Bryant said. "Everybody's grouped together, and it's a tight-knit thing."

Longhorn quarterback James Brown got a little loose-lipped this past summer in the wake of UT's 51-15 thumping of the Aggies last year in Austin. He had engaged the James Brown Frown before the game, where he checked out the Aggies' eyes.

"A&M looked kind of intimidated, actually," Brown said at the Big 12 football media day. "I don't know how you can explain seeing that in someone's eyes when they come out ... [but] they looked kind of timid, like they weren't ready to play."

Even mild-mannered Aggie quarterback Branndon Stewart had some fun with that one.

"I don't know what kind of power he has to read into people's eyes, but I don't try to do that kind of analysis before games," Stewart said, grinning. "I just worry about going out and playing."

Brown said the Aggies should be worried, despite Texas's 4-6 record.

"I read where we were two-digit underdogs," he said.

"But I think they know it's going to be a tough game. I like playing in big games and in televised games. And I don't like being picked to lose."

Aggie offensive lineman Chris Ruhman isn't a big fan of Brown's Frown.

"Tell him to come look in my eyes before this game," Ruhman said. "Quotes are quotes, and the tables are turned this year."

The coaches, both classy men who respect each other and are friends, aren't involved in the razzin' and ridiculin'. But neither Texas's John Mackovic or A&M's R.C. Slocum downplay the hype, either. Both said this week that, no matter the outcome, they have to live with it 364 days a year.

"If you're playing a backyard game, it's the pride of you against the guy you live next door to," Slocum said. "When you get to high school, it's you against the cross-town rival. And then you move on up, in the state of Texas, it's the big intrastate rivalry.

"Every function you go to with a mixed crowd, someone is bringing it up. Either some Aggie is bring-

Rosa Jolivet rode a train to aptly named College Station—just like the old days—for her recruiting visit.

ing it up or some Longhorn is bringing it up, or some Aggie with a Longhorn brother-in-law is bringing it up."

Said Mackovic, "On one day of the year, we are the most fiercely competitive rival to each other that anyone will see."

Ruhman's right, too. The tables are turned this season after A&M finished last year 6-6, with the embarrassing loss to Texas the dirt dessert. Fiebiger said a Longhorn victory would salvage Texas's season.

"This sounds stupid," he said, "but I'd rather go 1-10 and beat A&M than go 10-1 and lose to A&M."

After last season, Slocum didn't hunt for the first time in memory.

"I wouldn't have enjoyed it, anyway," he said.

A writer asked Slocum if he didn't want to handle a gun at that point.

"And I didn't want to get around any Aggies with guns, either," Slocum corrected with a grin.

So for the 104th time—in a game trumpeted from Dallas to Houston and Uvalde to Sweetwater and everywhere in between—here we go again. This game is a huge part of Texas culture, and the players know that.

Remember, though, their traditional smack talk through gritted teeth also usually includes a smile.

College Station—Really

The town of College Station earned its name from an old railroad depot. It's not that standout Rosa Jolivet, one of the best hurdlers in school history, was a big fan of history, but Brazos Valley historians had to appreciate the manner in which she traveled to College Station for her recruiting visit: by train.

Many athletes took a train ride to College Station from places like Houston and Dallas early in the 20th century, but Jolivet took her ride in the mid-1990s. A&M assistant track coach Abe Brown asked Jolivet if she wanted to fly in or take a train from Houston.

She chose the latter.

"I had never ridden one," she said, smiling.

So what was her most memorable moment from the historic train ride on the Amtrak route?

"Nothing," she said, laughing. "We had a [high school] basketball game the night before, so I slept the whole way there. It must have been a good ride, though, because I didn't wake up all the way there. It was real smooth. No bumps."

Flaming Roof Dive

Rugby may only be a club sport at Texas A&M, but the Aggie rugby team often earned the campus's attention for its spirited competition—on and off the pitch.

One player in particular from the late 1990s, Johnny Pooler, took rugby games away from the field to new heights—literally. Pooler, a gregarious sort who'd later become a lieutenant in the U.S. Marine Corps, perfected the "flaming roof dive" while a student at A&M.

Pooler became best known for this in Aggieland, along with sprinting the 40-yard dash in 4.5 seconds as a winger on the school's touted rugby team. The flaming roof dive usually occurred at rugby parties and involved Pooler, who was five foot nine and 175 pounds, stripping down to his altogether and climbing onto the roof of the get-together.

From there, chants of "Pooler! Pooler!" would begin, and the future military officer would stuff toilet paper between his legs—and then light it on fire. By the times the flames were licking at his chops, the "Pooler!" chants had grown to epic proportions, and the braver among the folks below would line up to catch Pooler, who'd then do his best Greg Louganis imitation from the lofty perch.

CHAPTER SIX

Straight from the Thoroughbreds' Mouths

Who better to recount some of the more memorable and humorous moments in Aggie athletics than the athletes? Here are a few of their anecdotes.

JIM STERLING
FOOTBALL, 1939-1941, DEFENSIVE AND OFFENSIVE END,
PANHANDLE

Hitchin' a Ride to Glory—
or at Least College Station

Jim Sterling still has the nightmares—the ones where he dreams he misses practice, is kicked off the Texas A&M football team, and has to return to the wheat fields of Panhandle, Texas. It never happened. Sterling in fact had a good career for the Aggies and played on the program's lone national championship team. But that never stopped the dreams.

And he played for A&M more than 60 years ago.

"It's my biggest nightmare, even to this day," Sterling said. "That was a very serious time in my life. We were children of the Depression, and the only way I could go to school was to play football. And the only way I could stay in school was to play football. I served in World War II and was in some tough situations, but I never dream about the Army.

"But I still have that dream about missing practice and getting cut from the team. Or I dream that I'm sitting on the bench and my name isn't called—it's really a strange thing. I guess the fact that the pressure was so great to stay in school and stay on the football team, it really made a dent in my mental capacity."

That doesn't mean all of Sterling's memories of playing football for the Aggies are solemn, and one more humorous anecdote involved legendary coach Homer Norton. It was during a practice at Kyle Field his sophomore year that Sterling made a tremendous blunder on an end-around block. As he was returning to the huddle, Coach Norton bounded up to him.

"Stick out your hand!" he commanded.

Sterling did as he was told. Coach Norton spit a big wad of chewing tobacco into Sterling's open palm.

Sterling stood there as Coach Norton turned to go back to the sideline, and then without giving it another thought, Sterling wiped the juicy tobacco chew right up the crotch of the coach's rear end.

"I guess I'll always wonder why in the hell I did that," Sterling said. "I was struggling to stay on the team and in the starting lineup, and that wasn't very conducive to doing those things."

Sterling, who then quickly turned away from the coach, said he never found out Norton's reaction to the impulsive gesture.

"I was too embarrassed to look at him," Sterling said, chuckling.

Norton, who was fighting what doctors diagnosed as a severe case of streptococcus for about 30 months leading up to the Aggies' title season, is still the only coach to win a football national championship at Texas A&M.

"Coach Norton was quite an unusual character—you never really got to know him," Sterling said. "The first year I was there he built this mobile tower over the football field, and that's where he coached from. By my sophomore year he had come down from the tower and was on the field."

Sterling played and lived in a different era, and not just on the football field. On many weekends, he'd hitchhike the 500 miles from College Station to Panhandle, which rests to the east of Amarillo.

"I was always back in school by Monday morning," he said, grinning. "I'd leave on Friday, get home late Friday night, stay Saturday with my folks, and on Sunday morning they'd take me down to the highway so I could get back to school. Looking back on all of that hitchhiking, now I wonder, 'How in the world did I do all of that? And why would I do it?' Maybe I don't have all of my faculties—or I didn't at that time, anyway."

One time he was hitching a ride back from Panhandle, when an elderly couple pulling a two-wheel trailer picked him up about 10 miles outside of Memphis, Texas.

"You see that trailer back there?" the elderly gentleman asked the strapping six-foot-two, 180-pound lad, once he was on board. "We need you to help us load it up at the mill."

So, Sterling dutifully used a big pitchfork to load a trailer-full of cottonseed for the couple and then went on about his way to College Station. After all, he had to be back in College Station that Monday morning for class—and back on the football field that afternoon for practice, so as not to get cut.

M.C. DOUGLASS
BASKETBALL AND GOLF, CLASS OF 1953, PAMPA

The Longest Shot

It was February 1950, and Douglass remembers it as if it was yesterday. Texas A&M versus Baylor in old DeWare Fieldhouse. He was on the A&M freshman basketball team, and his team had just finished playing the Baylor freshmen. The youngsters had a front-row seat to watch the varsity game that followed.

The varsity contest was dead even all the way. Over the years Douglass played in and witnessed dozens of basketball games that were decided by a last-second shot. But none in his mind was as memorable as this one.

Baylor had an opportunity to win the game in regulation, but missed a free throw. The game went into overtime. Time was running out when

Jewell McDowell wound up with the ball. He had just crossed midcourt on the right side.

The next few seconds seemed like an eternity. McDowell made a slight turn to look back at the clock, and then he turned and shot the ball with his old-timey two-handed set shot with about a second left. The ball seemed to float in the air forever, and just as it reached its peak, the crowd became very quiet and the buzzer sounded.

The ball arced down and hit nothing but net. The crowd went wild as A&M prevailed 56-54. Douglass had never seen a game where time just seemed to stand still during the final play.

Walter "Buddy" Davis, John DeWitt, Wally Moon, and McDowell, who were members of that team, all have been voted into the A&M Sports Hall of Fame for the many honors they achieved while in college.

JACK PARDEE
FOOTBALL, 1954-1956, LINEBACKER AND FULLBACK, CHRISTOVAL

A Different Game

Jack Pardee said the biggest change in football from the time he played it to now is the fact that it's grown into a game of specialists. He said the one-platoon system of yesteryear really hurt a lot of players who could have done wonderful things on one side of the ball—the offensive side of the ball.

Ken Hall, fullback for the Aggies in the mid-1950s, was a perfect example. Hall had set the national high school rushing record with 11,232 yards while at Sugar Land High, and he'd brought his bountiful abilities to Aggieland. He played fullback at A&M, and in coach Paul "Bear" Bryant's system, the fullback played linebacker—as Pardee did.

Only Hall was a spectacular running back who couldn't play linebacker very well.

"And Coach Bryant chose his team by how you played defense," said Pardee, who became an All-Pro linebacker in the NFL. "That really hurt Ken Hall and a lot of other players."

Hall averaged 2,808 rushing yards per season in high school and once rushed for 520 yards on 11 carries in a single game. His senior year at

Tough-as-nails Jack Pardee was one of Bear Bryant's favorites for Pardee's ability to excel on both sides of the ball.

Sugar Land, he rushed for 4,045 yards, catching the eye of Bryant and every other college coach for such eye-popping numbers.

Alas, Hall never even lettered at A&M because he wasn't very good at defense, and Bryant later told folks—and even Hall—he felt guilty that Hall's career never panned out in Aggieland.

John David Crow, a teammate of Pardee's and the school's only Heisman Trophy winner, agreed that football was a much different sport a half-century ago.

"If you came out of the ballgame, you couldn't go back in until the quarter changed," Crow said. "If you got dinged a little bit or even if you got hurt quite a bit, you were expected to suck it up and stay in the ballgame and play hurt.

"You'd also never come off the field and say you were tired. You see people today come off the field when they get a little winded—which makes the game quicker and faster and some would say better. Well, you just didn't do that back then, and that was the reason we practiced the way we practiced and got pushed the way we got pushed.

"The thought was the best-conditioned team would win. There wasn't any team that had 22 or 30 really good players. You put your 11 best guys out there and they played both ways."

That one-platoon system ended in the mid-1960s, paving the way for the almost constant substitutions of today.

> "MY DAD SAID IT WAS FOR RESIST-
> ANCE. LIKE IF SOMEONE WAS TRYING
> TO TACKLE YOU, YOU STILL KEPT
> YOUR FEET GOING. IT PAID OFF."
>
> —Chris Cole, A&M and NFL receiver on his dad tying a
> harness, tire, and some cement together for him
> to drag around the block while growing up

GENE STALLINGS
FOOTBALL, 1954-1956, DEFENSIVE AND OFFENSIVE END,
PARIS

Grinding It Out

Gene Stallings, who'd later coach Alabama to a national championship, was considered tough as nails, just like many of his teammates of that day, but even Stallings grimaced that fall day in 1956 when trainer Smokey Harper forgot the team's mouthpieces on a trip to Baylor.

"Of all the places," Stallings said, laughing. "Baylor was tough. When you got through playing Baylor in those days, you were beat up, so that wasn't the place to leave the mouth guards at home. But we just played without 'em."

But maybe the old adage that what doesn't hurt you—or make you gnash your teeth more than you'd like—makes you tougher was true.

The Aggies won their first Southwest Conference title in 15 years in 1956 and defeated rival Texas in Memorial Stadium, which opened in 1924, for the first time in history. Oh, and by the way, they also defeated Baylor 19-13 that year, sans mouthpieces.

JOHN DAVID CROW
FOOTBALL, 1955-1957, RUNNING BACK,
SPRINGHILL, LOUISIANA

The Man's Presence

Coach Paul "Bear" Bryant heavily recruited John David Crow out of Louisiana and finally won the star back over in the spring of 1954.

Crow, who would become Bryant's only Heisman Trophy winner, quickly realized he would play his college ball for a man who commanded respect, even by simply walking a door.

"When Coach Bryant walked in a room, everything got quiet," Crow said. "There was this door on this room the team always met in down under the stadium. We met there before just about every practice.

"We could all be sitting in the room with our backs to that door, and people would be coming and going and so forth. But when Coach Bryant walked in, just the way the door squeaked when he opened it, the room would become stone silent."

A dozen years later, Crow served as an assistant to Bryant at Alabama. Crow was opening an account at a bank in Tuscaloosa, Alabama, when the bank owner approached him. The man offered Crow his hand, and the two began talking about Coach Bryant.

"I brought up the fact that it was still the same way as it had been at A&M, that when Coach Bryant walked in the room everything got quiet," Crow said. "He told me, 'Hell, John, Coach Bryant is on the board of this bank, and I walk in the meeting room and all of the directors are shooting the bull and carrying on and so forth, but he walks in there and everybody gets stone silent.

"'Including me, and I own the damn bank!'"

Natural Conditioning

Crow said over the years people have made a big deal of the fact that Bryant didn't allow water during his brutal practices—gulping down the thirst-quencher was considered a sign of weakness—but Crow said that wasn't uncommon among plenty of coaches of that era.

"I'm not saying our group was tougher than anyone else, but times were different," Crow said. "We were used to sleeping without air conditioning, and if you wanted to get cool, you went outside and sat under a shade tree. You didn't sit in the house.

"It seems to me your body would be more accustomed to heat back then than it would be today. Now, players go out of their air-conditioned houses and get in their air-conditioned cars, and drive to their air-conditioned dressing rooms, and then get out on the field.

"I think that's one of the reasons why there weren't more heat-related deaths back in those days—water or no water."

HUGH McELROY
FOOTBALL, 1970-1971, RECEIVER, HOUSTON

Ties That Bind

Hugh McElroy learned to really appreciate Kyle Field and all it represented after his playing days.

"At the time, it really wasn't that special to me, because I didn't know much about A&M or its history—I wasn't a legacy or anything," said McElroy, the first African-American in history to start and score a touchdown for the Aggies.

"But I can recall the first time I attended a game after I had graduated, and for the first time I actually saw the Aggie Band perform at halftime. That was a big deal. That was a real big deal."

After that, McElroy began religiously attending the revered A&M traditions of Silver Taps and Aggie Muster, honoring the Aggie dead.

"That's when I really started thinking about the history of the university and what it is among us that ties people from so many different walks of life together," he said. "We don't know anything about each other, really, except that we share this common bond—and then it really starts to mean something and makes you proud to be a member of the Aggie family."

JOHN THORNTON
BASKETBALL, 1974-1975, SAN ANTONIO

Wrong Way

John Thornton was by former coach and lifetime comedian Shelby Metcalf's side for many years, first as a player and then as an assistant coach. Thornton, who now serves as a senior associate athletic director at A&M, humorously recalled that teammate Webb Williams (1973-1975) once heaved up an outside shot, and Metcalf yelled, "Get in for Webb!"

Ray Roberts, who was seated on the bench next to Metcalf, jumped up and ran to the scorer's table. Metcalf glanced over at the excited Roberts.

"Ray," the coach said, shaking his head, "I was talking to the ball."

The Texas A&M Temptations

Metcalf once bought the team matching leisure suits, complete with wide collars and bell-bottoms.

"Back in the old days, you could provide your players with travel wear like those leisure suits," Thornton said. "These suits were supposed to be maroon, but they were more red than anything. Shelby was extremely superstitious, so we all had to wear the same thing. We looked like the Temptations.

"Shelby would wear the suit, right along with everyone else. The suits were made of polyester, and they would get runs in them, but he'd still make us wear them, runs and all. Because we were winning with them."

Out of Control

Arkansas's Barnhill Arena was one of the most intimidating atmospheres to play in, and one time in the mid-1980s the Aggies visited when both programs were playing pretty well and when Thornton was an assistant coach for A&M.

Arkansas coach Eddie Sutton immediately started trying to intimidate the officials, and he received a technical early on. So did Aggie coach Shelby Metcalf.

"Moose" Stubing was the head official, and in a side note, an assistant coach for the California Angels. The game was quickly getting out of control, and Eddie and Shelby finally were jaw to jaw.

"Both of y'all settle down," Stubing told the coaches, before turning to Metcalf. "Shelby, I'm taking control of this game. I'll get it in order."

The game started back up and things quickly went sour for the Aggies—as one bad thing after another happened and Arkansas opened a big lead.

"Moose ran by and Shelby caught his attention," Thornton said, grinning. "Shelby yelled, 'Hey, Moose, I liked it better when it was out of control!'"

Worst Turns First

In 1987 the Aggies were in a tailspin and couldn't seem to beat anybody. They wound up the No. 8 and last seed in the Southwest Conference basketball tournament and drew No. 1 seed TCU in the first round.

"When you're the eighth seed, you get the worst accommodations and earliest practices times," Thornton said. "We had a 10 a.m. practice time the day before the game at Reunion Arena in Dallas.

"Shelby was mad because we had underachieved and the season hadn't gone our way. So we actually got up at 5 a.m. and bussed from College Station to Dallas the same day of the early practice. Anyone else would have gotten there the night before."

When the sleepy-eyed Aggies arrived at Reunion, there had been a concert the night before, and trucks were backed up to the place and were in the way as workers loaded up the concert equipment.

So, under those circumstances, the Aggies put their hands in the huddle and were just about to break for practice. That's when gregarious guard Todd Holloway waved off the break with a few immortal words.

"Wait a minute, man, wait a minute," Holloway said, grimacing. "Come on, man. They're treating us like we're Rice or something."

Thus inspired by Holloway's harsh yet accurate assessment, the Aggies won the league tournament as its last seed.

"I feel very foolish," Metcalf said afterward. "I should have gone to Las Vegas this week instead of wasting my time on a basketball tournament."

In a touching moment, the coach then added, "Our players can look back at this later in life and realize anything is possible."

JACOB GREEN
FOOTBALL, 1977-1979, DEFENSIVE END, HOUSTON

The Frats Versus the Unreals —and Tony Franklin

Jacob Green was among the second wave of African-American football players to play for Texas A&M, and he and some of his fellow recruits and teammates quickly noticed something was missing in Aggieland.

"Back then we didn't really have any fraternities for black athletes," he said. "So we made up our own. We called ourselves the Frats. [Defensive back] Lester Hayes came up with his own group—the Unreals.

"We would sit around and talk noise and play pool and do all kinds of crazy stuff that college guys do. We'd talk a lot of noise about the Unreals, because we were the Frats."

The Unreals also took Caucasian kicker Tony Franklin, one of the most prolific at his position in the history of college football, under their wings.

"Tony, he was an adopted Unreal," Green said, grinning.

Franklin set 18 NCAA records in his time in Aggieland, and once kicked field goals of 64 and 65 yards against Baylor—in the same game.

Pat Thomas, A&M's first African-American All-American as a defensive back in the mid-1970s, remembers being in awe of Franklin's powerful leg.

"Tony was a rare individual, and a rare kicker," Thomas said. "He was one of the first barefoot kickers to come through the Southwest Conference, so he got a lot of notoriety because of that. With a good defense, a running game, and kicker like Tony, we could really control field position during a game."

SHAWN ANDAYA
SOFTBALL, 1984-1987, PITCHER, STOCKTON, CALIFORNIA

National Champions

Texas A&M has won three NCAA national championships in all of its team sports, and the Aggie softball team owns two of those titles.

And Shawn Andaya, as a senior in 1987, pitched a perfect game in one of the title contests. Andaya, one of the most decorated athletes to play A&M's most successful team sport, cheerfully recalled a few vivid moments from the 1987 softball world series in Omaha, Nebraska.

"A representative from the Aggie softball team was asked to say the prayer at the All-American banquet," Andaya said. "Zina Ochoa did so with grace."

Then Andaya recounted the rest of the story. Ochoa finished the prayer with the obligatory "Amen," and then abruptly tagged on, "See ya in the finals!"

"Our whole team cracked up, and lucky for us, we actually made the finals," Andaya said, grinning. "And we won."

That May weekend the Aggies had to defeat UCLA twice to win the national title. In the first contest, Andaya hurled a perfect game in a 1-0 A&M victory. Andaya also pitched the second game, and the Aggies emerged victorious 4-1 against the Bruins. A&M had finished as national runner-up two of the three previous years.

"It seemed like the impossible dream," Andaya said. "I remember riding over in the team van, and just thinking, 'This is crazy. We've got to win two against UCLA. Why do I even have this dream?' But we had a lot of spirit on that team."

The Coach

Coach Bob Brock, who had led the Aggies to a previous NCAA national title in 1983, served as the Aggies' taskmaster.

"It was very difficult sometimes to keep a straight face when Coach Brock was lecturing us for not playing well or not being mentally into the game, especially one time when a ladybug landed on his mustache and wouldn't fly away," Andaya said, laughing. "We got nothing out of that lecture."

Andaya also served as an assistant coach under Brock—a squat, stocky man with a deeply tanned face and big brown mustache—following her playing days. She recalled one time when a player, Barbi Tuck, showed up 45 minutes late for practice.

As Tuck came in, Andaya and Coach Brock glanced at her.

"Where the hell have you been?" Coach Brock asked.

"In my room," she said.

"Doing what?" he asked.

"Watching *Oprah*," she replied.

Andaya couldn't help but giggle at Tuck's brutally honest answer. Brock told Tuck to start running and he'd tell her when to stop—and Andaya said the poor girl finally stopped some time that season.

Luby's Aficionado

Brock loved to eat at cafeterias when the team was on the road, even if the players didn't.

On one trip to Louisiana, Brock promised the hungry players, who were bothering him to eat, that he had a great place in mind, and that they were almost there.

"Sure enough, we pulled up to a mall and there was a Luby's," Andaya said. "Coach was excited. He said, 'All right, girls, here we are!' He hopped off the bus, but everyone else just sat there. We refused to move. After going into the cafeteria and then coming back out and climbing on the bus, Coach was livid.

"Later on, we ate at Chili's. It's that type of strong will that makes you win!"

Jersey Girl

Andaya remembers when All-American Cindy Cooper once forgot her jersey when the team was playing at McNeese State one season. The team manager had slipped her another jersey—without her usual number—and as Coach Brock hit her grounders he realized something was amiss.

"Where's your regular jersey?" he asked.

"In College Station," she said.

"What's it doing there?" he continued.

"Hanging up on a hanger in the closet," she replied.

The veins in Brock's head started bulging, and he sat his All-American for an entire doubleheader.

Extreme Focus

Here's how intent the team was on winning a national championship in 1987: The players gave up snacks and caffeine because they didn't want to test positive for anything—*anything*—following the world series.

"There was a lot of drug testing going on at that time, and we were so paranoid of testing positive for something that we stopped eating chocolate and drinking sodas and alcohol," Andaya said. "After winning the national championship and before leaving the ballpark, our parents awarded us with huge bags of M&M's and Snickers, and we washed the candy down with soda. Yummy!"

RICHMOND WEBB
FOOTBALL, 1986-1989, TACKLE AND GUARD, DALLAS

The Gunner and The Runner

Richmond Webb had the pleasure of protecting the blind sides of two mightily different but beloved quarterbacks in Miami Dolphins All-Pro Dan Marino and Texas A&M's Bucky Richardson.

"Dan was known for his fourth-quarter comebacks, and if we were down and had 60 or 80 yards to go for a touchdown late in the game, you could actually see a change in him—in his eyes and in his voice,"

Webb said. "He would tell you that we were going to get it done, and you actually believed you were going to get it done. He had that gift."

But in the years before Webb became a Pro Bowler guarding Marino, he protected Richardson in Aggieland. Richardson earned All-Conference honors and the Aggie Heart Award in his time at A&M.

"Bucky was the kind of guy who you'd think was about to pitch the ball, and the next thing you know he would tuck it and run the ball like a running back," Webb said. "He was one of the toughest guys I ever played with.

"The quarterback is the leader in the huddle, and if anybody sees where he might have any doubt in his mind, it affects the whole group. It's when times get tough that you find your true leaders, and both Dan and Bucky were that kind of quarterback."

QUENTIN CORYATT
FOOTBALL, 1990-1991, LINEBACKER, BAYTOWN

No Boos Allowed

Some of Quentin Coryatt's favorite moments as arguably the most intimidating linebacker to ever don the maroon and white were those precious minutes before kickoff at Kyle Field.

"Once you stepped foot into that weight room, you knew that it was game time," he said. "Then you ran out onto the field, and there was nothing like it, because the band was playing 'The Aggie War Hymn,' and the fans were just going crazy.

"It was comforting to know, too, that when the chips were down, you weren't going to hear a boo. You weren't going to hear anything negative from the fans—win, lose, or draw. You knew the crowd was on your side, and was the last wall of defense."

Coryatt, who'd later be the No. 2 overall selection in the 1992 NFL draft, gained most of his notoriety at A&M for breaking TCU receiver Kyle McPherson's jaw in three places in what's affectionately known around Aggieland as "The Hit."

"The Hit" was legal, and it left McPherson with his jaw wired shut for the next two months. And many observers considered him lucky.

LISA BRANCH
BASKETBALL, 1993-1996, GUARD, DeSOTO

A Total Trip

Lisa Branch was the best, most nimble women's basketball player to come through Texas A&M, but even she had an awkward moment or two—and one came before a large crowd at G. Rollie White Coliseum her senior year.

The Aggies, who were having a down season at that point, were hosting high-flying Texas Tech.

"We were running through our warmups and were all really excited about playing the Lady Raiders, and one of my teammates accidentally tripped me," Branch said. "I just fell flat on the floor in front of all of those people. I didn't know what to do, except to laugh."

Later on in the same game, with the Aggies trailing Tech, A&M assistant coach Kristy Sims (now Curry) went to take a seat during halftime, only to also fall during a tongue-lashing of the players in the locker room.

"Of course, everybody looked at me, and I'm terrible about holding in my laughs," Branch said. "So everybody started laughing."

Tech won that game, but A&M, which finished fourth in regular-season league play in 1996, earned the last laugh that season in the Southwest Conference. The Aggies defeated Rice, powerhouse Texas, and, yes, Texas Tech, to claim the final SWC tournament title.

"I'll always remember in the second round against Texas, that the Tech fans started cheering for us," Branch said. "There was all of that red and black in the stands, cheering for us. They thought they had a better chance of beating us than Texas."

Branch, A&M's all-time leader in points and assists, became the school's first All-American in women's basketball. She could have attended a more established program out of DeSoto High, but instead chose to make her mark on the fledgling Aggies, who made the NCAA's Sweet Sixteen her sophomore season.

"Growing up, I was always one to root for the underdog," Branch said. "I wanted to be a giant killer, and that's why I chose A&M. Texas had a legacy, and Tech was on the rise, and I wanted to be one of the players who took those teams down."

KRISTIE SMEDSRUD
VOLLEYBALL, 1994-1997, OUTSIDE HITTER,
SAN DIEGO, CALIFORNIA

Lure of the Yells

Coming from California for her recruiting trip in 1993, Kristie Smedsrud had no idea what Texas A&M was all about. During her visit she attended an Aggie football game and was awestruck by the school's famous yells and hand signals.

"I'd never seen anything like that in my life," Smedsrud said. "Then we went to a volleyball game, and the crowd did the same thing."

Smedsrud quickly made up her mind about where she would attend college, despite her West Coast upbringing.

"I knew there wasn't going to be any other school in the country that was going to be as unique as Texas A&M," she said. "I fell in love with the place in five minutes."

Maybe the only thing more unique than A&M was Smedsrud's energetic teammate, Stacy Sykora. For years, the two formed the Southwest Conference's and then the Big 12's most formidable outside-hitting duo.

"She would blare rap music in the locker room and was just a phenomenal dancer, and Michael Jackson was her specialty," Smedsrud said. "She would do The Moonwalk and the whole bit."

So one night the team went dancing in College Station and, sure enough, late in the evening a Michael Jackson tune blared from the speakers.

"It was like the sea parted and everyone in the club just backed away and formed a circle around her," Smedsrud said. "I've never seen anybody draw a crowd like that before."

Four years after her arrival at A&M, Smedsrud departed as one of the program's top all-time players.

"Texas A&M was more than I could have imagined," said Smedsrud, who returned to the West Coast and works at San Diego State University. "I couldn't have asked for a more supportive community and a better academic setting. I brag about that all of the time. People get tired of hearing my A&M stories, but I can't imagine having gone to school anywhere else."

HUNTER GOODWIN
FOOTBALL, 1994-1995, OFFENSIVE LINEMAN, BELLVILLE

The Rivalry

Hunter Goodwin couldn't believe his eyes that cold November day in 1993 in Netum Steed training complex next to Kyle Field.

Goodwin was redshirting for the Aggies that season after transferring from Texas A&M–Kingsville. He'd grow into an All-Conference offensive lineman and play eight years in the NFL as a tight end, but at that time he was taking in the scene in the hours and minutes before A&M kicked off against rival Texas.

"That was when the realization hit me of the hatred that particular group of guys had for Texas," Goodwin said. "There was a core group that had an absolute disdain for the teasips."

Goodwin said that gang included linemen Chris Dausin, Lance Teichelman, Eric England, and Sam Adams.

"It left an image in my mind about how I was supposed to feel about Texas," Goodwin said. "Before the game the team was in Netum Steed, warming up, and there were a bunch of recruits and their parents in there. With some of the language being used and some of the things being said, when you looked in the eyes of those parents, the fear you saw was the same as if someone had pulled a gun on you. It was that intense.

"You could definitely tell this wasn't just another game day. There was something different going on—it was almost like it was personal."

Goodwin said the team's then-recruiting coordinator Tim Cassidy calmly walked over to Dausin and asked him to tone it down in front of the recruits and their parents. Dausin, already raging with kickoff just around the corner, wanted no part of such sensitivity.

"If they don't like what the f— what I'm saying," Dausin screamed without missing a beat, "they can get the f— out!"

Goodwin said he doesn't know in this new era of multimedia, websites, seven-on-seven camps, and multiple all-star games, if the rivalry will ever be what it once was between the schools.

"Today the players on opposing teams develop relationships," Goodwin said. "It can be hard to hate someone you know. All of those things have changed the face of the game. Back then the only way you got to know somebody is if you were on the same recruiting trip as that guy.

"It's easier to hate the unknown."

MYA TRUELOVE
SOFTBALL, 1994-1997, FIRST BASEMAN, DEER PARK

Wipe Out

While the Texas A&M–Texas rivalry was at least 100 years old in some other sports, in the spring of 1997 it was brand new in one sport: softball.

Mya Truelove, owner of one of the most unique names in college sports, and teammate Gina Perez made sure one Sunday in Austin that there would be no love lost between the programs. A&M, an established softball program, crushed the Longhorns 9-0 in a game called after six innings because of the run rule.

A huge chalk Longhorn symbol in the dirt behind the pitching mound also had caught the Aggies' eyes in the midst of the whipping—and they quickly began plotting ways to "saw Varsity's horns off," as "The Aggie War Hymn" intones.

"During the game, Gina would run out to play center field and she would kick through the symbol every time—she would just drag her foot through it," Truelove said.

And every time, UT player Nikki Cockrell—who had transferred from A&M—would try and straighten it out the next inning. Finally, the game mercifully ended for the Longhorns.

"Gina and I had agreed that she would run in from center and I would run over from first, and we would wipe out the Horns on each side," Truelove said, grinning. "We called it a 'swipe and run.' We got a few not-so-nice looks from the Longhorns, but, hey, that's what the rivalry is all about, right?"

Surreal Setting for Sprints

A more poignant moment for Truelove came during one of the team's 6 a.m. offseason workouts under former coach Bob Brock.

"We would run on Kyle Field, and one November morning the Aggie Band was out there practicing at that time," Truelove said. "So it was the Aggie softball team and the Aggie Band on each side of the 50-yard line. It was totally dark outside, except for the lights of Kyle, and there was a mist on the turf.

"We were running sprints and doing agility drills while the band was playing 'The Aggie War Hymn' at 6 a.m., and it's a surreal moment I'll never forget. It was the only time we ever enjoyed one of those morning workouts."

DAT NGUYEN
FOOTBALL, 1995-1998, LINEBACKER, ROCKPORT

A Bit Late—or Way Early

College Station was a fun town to go out in for Dat Nguyen, because of the friendliness of Aggieland. But it was fun to have some parties at the ol' apartments, too, he said.

So that's what Nguyen, Texas A&M's all-time leading tackler, did one night in the spring of 1998—he had a party at the Treehouse Apartments that are just south of campus. Just about every football player on the team was there that night. Nguyen's roommate, Les Casterline, was celebrating his birthday, which seemed like a good enough reason to have a party.

One of the players started feeding Casterline drinks and in the party Casterline had passed out—even though the gang was supposed to go out on the town a little later on. So, because the party's star attraction was fast asleep, none of the rest of the birthday partiers went out.

At 7 a.m. the next morning, Casterline sprang to his feet and yelled, "Hey, everybody, time to go out!" People just shook their heads.

"What? It's only 7," he said, glancing at the clock.

He thought it was still 7 p.m. Some birthday, huh? So one of Nguyen's funniest memories of a night out on the town is one that never actually happened.

JOHN SCHESCHUK
BASEBALL, 1995-1999, FIRST BASEMAN, PASADENA

Tarp Slide for Diapers

In 1997 the Aggies were in a rain delay at Olsen Field and it was just pouring down, so athletic field manager Leo Goertz and his crew got out the tarp to cover the field.

The baseball team was sitting in the dugout when one of the fellows glanced down at left-handed pitcher Shane King, a brash and funny guy and a great teammate to have, Scheschuk said. King wouldn't have cared if he was facing the New York Yankees—he thought he was the best pitcher out there, no matter the situation, Scheschuk added.

That's why the Aggies figured in the middle of a monotonous rain delay, the lefty would be perfect for a few shenanigans.

"King," one of his teammates said as the rest nodded their approval, "I dare you to do a tarp slide."

King glanced back at the rest of the fellows and raised his eyebrows.

"I'll do it for 40 bucks," he said.

So the players gathered the funds and held on to the money, and King strolled out of the dugout in full uniform and into the pouring rain. He even forgot to take off his belt, which could have sliced the tarp. So, belt and all, he dashed full blast across the infield and all the way to second base, and belly-flopped right in the middle of the tarp—sliding in merriment to the roars of the dugout.

The players couldn't believe it. King, who already was married with child while playing college baseball, returned to the dugout, soaked and smiling.

"Boys," he said, "that's three weeks' worth of diapers I just earned. Pay up."

Love for the Glove

Second baseman Brian Benefield was a big glove guy—his glove was always immaculate and perfectly formed, and he'd treat it like royalty. So, because of that, Scheschuk recalled, one time pitcher John Sneed, a big guy at six foot six, stuffed Benefield's glove under a water cooler in the dugout. Sneed then plopped down on the cooler, put all of his weight on it, and wiggled around—absolutely mangling Benefield's prized posses-sion to the snickers of his teammates.

Wiener Toss

Olsen Field was famous for its quarter hot dog nights. The players would load up on the sweet deals, as well, because as college students, they usually didn't have any money.

So early in one game on quarter hot dog night, Scheschuk remem-bers, shortstop Richard Petru was cruising out to his position and stick-ing his fingers in his glove—but his digits didn't get very far. Petru, a team favorite and a good-natured sort, found five wieners stuck up the finger holes in his glove. He scrambled to toss the wieners aside on the infield before the inning started.

> "IT'S LIKE THAT OL' BOY USED TO SAY, 'I LOVE IT WHEN A PLAN COMES TOGETHER.'"
>
> —*Former A&M defensive line coach Bill Johnson, referencing the 1980s hit TV show* The A-Team

CHAPTER SEVEN

Playing the Field

Texas A&M athletics is home of two of the most revered "fields" in college sports: football's Kyle Field and baseball's Olsen Field. Below are a few tales from the fields and within the historic walls rising around them, along with several tender reminisces about old G. Rollie White Coliseum.

Leo Goertz

Leo Goertz's work hours are easy—to explain.

"He works from when he can to when he can't," said Billy Pickard, Texas A&M associate athletic director for facilities.

Goertz has served as A&M's athletics field manager since 1996. It's fitting that at agriculturally rich A&M, Goertz works farmers' hours, in maintaining the immaculate grass of the Aggies' many playing surfaces.

"If Leo were to leave here, they'd have to hire two or three people to take his place," former basketball coach Mark Johnson said.

Goertz is simply a man married to the soil, something he's been a part of at A&M since he arrived as a freshman in 1978, the same year Olsen Field opened. Goertz's job description includes maintaining the surfaces of Kyle Field, the grass football practice fields, the Anderson track complex, and the softball and soccer fields along with Olsen.

"We've gone from about three acres in 20 years to almost 20 acres of natural turf," Goertz said.

Goertz's own dimensions—six foot four and 295 pounds—make him sound like an offensive lineman, and his deeply tanned skin and mainstay Oakley sunglasses—the huge waterhose typically draped over his shoulder doesn't hurt—make him an instantly recognizable figure at Olsen.

But Goertz also is well known around the state and even the nation, because he's recognized for his soil expertise. He speaks at clinics around the country about field maintenance. At the clinics and especially in Aggieland, Goertz is a one-name wonder—in the mold of Madonna or Shaq. Everyone knows who Leo is.

"He's the nicest guy in the field," said assistant athletic field manager Craig Potts, pun possibly intended. "It's amazing how many people he knows."

Goertz is a New Braunfels native who said he "didn't know Bermuda grass from rye grass" when he arrived at A&M in 1978. But he approached then-Aggie baseball coach Tom Chandler about working at Olsen and has been at it ever since. The Goertz family farmed in New Braunfels, and Goertz's interest in soil never waned.

"It just came natural," he said. "I could never sit behind a desk and push a pencil. One of the fun things about this business is you never know what the next day is going to bring. The weather is either your best friend or your biggest foe. Every day is a new challenge."

Billy and the Bear

Billy Pickard opens the door to the men's restroom on the ground level of the west side of Kyle Field and invites you on a quick tour of a touch of Texas A&M football history. Odd, but true, according to Pickard, who likely has spent more time at Kyle Field—where the Aggies began playing football in 1906—than anyone, living or dead.

Yes, sir, follow Pickard along the long troughs to the right, and when arriving at the last one, turn to the left, and behold. See that old doorframe straight ahead, the one now sealed off in white blocks and surrounded by the faded, old yellow bricks?

That's the one-time entrance—enclosed a couple of decades ago when Kyle's old meeting rooms were converted into restrooms—into coach Paul "Bear" Bryant's office. Imagine the revered coach sitting there. Picture him as a relatively young man, considering he was in his early 40s when he coached at A&M from 1954 to 1957.

Now envision Bryant, who would later win six national championships at Alabama, two days following his first game as Aggies coach, a 41-9 loss to Texas Tech in September 1954.

"We're going to take up where we left off against Tech!" a furious Bryant said, hammering a football down on the 20-yard line in the stifling heat of late summer.

"Toughest practice I can remember," said former A&M end Gene Stallings, who had survived an unexpected training camp in Junction a few weeks before. Bryant took 110 players to Junction, and only 35—including Stallings—returned.

Pickard witnessed Bryant's coaching methods as a student trainer at A&M in the 1950s. He's also observed coaches Jim Myers, Hank Foldberg, Stallings, Emory Bellard, Tom Wilson, Jackie Sherrill, and R.C. Slocum all run the A&M program.

That's why A&M fans should get a thrill out of what Pickard said about current coach Dennis Franchione, hired from Alabama in 2002.

"I've had the good fortune to be around some great people and some great coaches," said Pickard, A&M's director of athletic facilities. "But I've never been around a coach who can concentrate and focus on what he's doing on the field like Coach Fran. I've never seen anything like it."

Bryant's players, for all of his toughness and gruffness toward them, would have busted through the white brick that now seals off the original door to his Kyle Field office to please him. Early in his career at A&M, it seemed Franchione was developing his own allegiance among the players, even with his tough-love ways.

Following the team's first summer practice, Franchione spoke of developing a toughness that would translate into more successful fourth quarters. Bryant, too, usually spoke in terms of fourth quarters during his sometimes brutal practices, when his players' parched tongues stuck past their bone-dry lips.

"There are two ingredients that go into fourth-quarter failures," Franchione said. "One is physical, and the other is mental. We have to get mentally tough and have the ability to focus when we get tired and hot."

Billy Pickard has spent more time in and around Kyle Field than anyone in history.

As Franchione spoke, his exhausted players file by, dangling tongues in search of a little Gatorade. Bear Bryant, by all accounts, likely would have nodded approvingly.

The Holler House

Funny how four walls and some hardwood can create so many memories. After 44 years of Aggie basketball old G. Rollie White Coliseum—the "Holler House on the Brazos"—closed its doors to hoops forever following the 1998 season.

Here are some memories from a few folks who spent time in the unforgettable old haunt:

Reid Gettys, lifetime member of the University of Houston's famed Phi Slama Jama: "When we would come here [on a team that included future NBA Hall of Famers Hakeem Olajuwon and Clyde Drexler] there would be Aggies hanging from the rafters. The fans were right on top of you, and G. Rollie White had the old metal lockers and was cold and drafty. I loved it.

"When I was a sophomore, I was the first one out of the locker room, and I wasn't up on my Aggie traditions. And there's this dog [Reveille] in the middle of the floor [defecating], and people are just standing there and watching. I thought, 'Why doesn't someone get that mutt off the floor?'"

Lynn Hickey, former A&M women's basketball coach: "When we had our offices up there, the animal problem got to be interesting. When we'd watch videotape at night, we had to keep our feet in chairs because of the mice that would come out of the walls.

"We'd get raccoons coming out of the ceiling. The trees were so close to the windows the squirrels would crawl in, and we used to have some screaming ladies up there trying to get those squirrels back outside.

"Before we put in the new floor [in the 1990s], you had to get something to knock the nails down on the floor. The best memories were those big wins against Texas Tech, Texas, and Florida the year Lisa Branch was a sophomore [in 1994]. The crowd was into it, and people were running on the floor after the game.

"When I walk down those ramps, I still get goose bumps, because I spent so many hours in there, it's kind of like home."

Bill Little, Texas assistant athletic director: "I remember the Aggie Band and the sound that it created in there. G. Rollie White was an atmosphere that was always wonderful to play in because people were so involved in the game. And whether or not you were home or visitor, you got caught up in that. It helped the opponent as much as the Aggies sometimes. Abe Lemons and Shelby Metcalf had some real battles in there."

Brad Marquardt, A&M assistant sports information director: "G. Rollie White has a special place in my heart, because I asked my wife [the former Wendy Smith] to marry me there. The night we met we went up there and played basketball real late, so it was kind of a special place for us." (The night of the proposal the two danced to "Unchained Melody" at midcourt before Marquardt took a knee.)

Randy Matson, former player (1966): "In those days [the late 1960s] most of the home conference games were sold out, and it was so loud in there. We would call a timeout, and Coach Metcalf would tell us what we were supposed to do. I'd ask [guard] Eddie Dominguez, 'What did he say?' and Eddie would respond, 'I don't know. I didn't hear a word. Grab somebody and guard 'em.'"

Marsha Sharp, the legendary Texas Tech women's basketball coach: "You always think about that sound echoing off the tin walls before they put in the [acoustics]. Obviously it was a little bit scary, too, when you had a dog [Reveille] nipping at your heels and chasing you off the court."

Billy Pickard, associate athletic director for facilities: "I remember the day we moved in [in 1954]. It was the most magnificent building. It was much better than Gregory Gym [in Austin]. You stood in awe because it was the biggest place we'd ever seen. The building is still in good shape for volleyball. I don't know how many people have asked me, 'When are we going to tear it down?' Why would you want to tear it down? That's a great building!"

Eddie Sutton, the legendary Arkansas and Oklahoma State coach: "We made 11 trips when I was coach of the Razorbacks, and we had some great battles with Shelby Metcalf. When you came into the arena, Reveille was always right there barking her head off. I think they taught her not to like any of the visiting coaches. At that time, the place would be packed, and they'd start that wave motion [sawing Varsity's horns off], and if you looked over there, you'd get motion sickness."

John Thornton, A&M assistant athletic director and former player (1974-1975): "One of the best memories was when we beat Arkansas on a last-second shot in 1975 [8,608 fans packed the house while another 1,700 watched across the way at Rudder Tower on closed-circuit television]. When the place was packed, I'll always remember sitting in the locker room and having a sense for the atmosphere outside because you could hear everything through those walls."

> "I REMEMBER WHEN THE GYM WAS BUILT. IT WASN'T A BAD PLACE TO PLAY. BUT THE TOWN IS KIND OF HARD TO GET TO. THEY NEED TO MOVE THE TOWN AND LEAVE THE GYM WHERE IT IS."
>
> —*Former Texas coach Abe Lemons on the closing of old G. Rollie White Coliseum to basketball*

A Glorious Old Trophy

Deep in the musty bowels of Kyle Field, in a small storage room at the end of a long, dark hallway—buried at the bottom of an old box—a sliver of lost treasure glimmered at Matt Watson.

As Texas A&M's football equipment manager, Watson didn't quite know what to think when he happened across the relic in the winter of 2004 while searching for old trophies to help fill out a glass case in the Aggies' new athletics building. From the top, the trophy looked like an old cup, tucked among other dusty artifacts from glory days long past and mostly forgotten.

Long past, in this case. But to Aggies everywhere, not forgotten. Watson lifted the grimy, sterling silver trophy—shaped like a fancy sugar bowl—and read the engraving: "To the Brilliant Victor of the 1940 Sugar Bowl Classic. Texas A&M 14, Tulane 13. New Orleans, January 1, 1940."

Watson rubbed his eyes, at first disbelieving the etching. He had discovered arguably the most precious piece of metal associated with A&M football.

"I didn't even know that trophy existed," Watson said of his find.

Members of A&M's 1939 football team—the only one in school history to win a national championship—certainly knew the cup existed. Sixty-five seasons before, on a joyous train ride home from New Orleans, they passed it around in celebration of a bowl victory, a perfect record, and a perfect season.

The cup was A&M's award for winning the Sugar Bowl, the final step in the Aggies' national title run. Not long after the train pulled into College Station, however, the trophy became an afterthought as the Aggies and others of their generation turned their thoughts from football to Adolf Hitler and war.

"People had their minds on things other than athletics," said Jim Sterling, 83, a member of the 1939 A&M team.

Somehow—no one's quite sure how—the trophy wound up at the bottom of a box in the back of a closet.

"When you're a young fellow, you don't really give a damn about something like that trophy," said Roy Bucek, another member of the 1939 team. "Coaches and athletic directors come and go, and somebody must have just forgot about it."

Today trophies seem to far outweigh—literally—their worth. A&M officials haven't been able to find shelf space for the jumbo trophy awarded to the Aggies in 2001 for winning a third-tier bowl named for a Houston furniture company. Yet, early last century, a foot-tall silver cup suited a national champion just fine.

"It's simple elegance," Watson said.

And some of the players, with a wink, saw the re-emergence of the school's Sugar Bowl championship trophy as a positive omen in a bid for regaining national prominence. Since 1939, the Aggies have finished as high as fifth in the final national rankings only once, that under legendary coach Paul "Bear" Bryant in 1956.

"I'm a real superstitious guy," A&M guard Aldo De La Garza said, "so maybe this will help us."

"Maybe," then-tackle Geoff Hangartner said with a smile, "it's a sign from God."

The cup now rests behind glass in the A&M lettermen's lounge. Cathy Capps of the lettermen's association said she hopes the trophy

Matt Watson clutches the Sugar Bowl trophy he found in a cardboard box in the bowels of Kyle Field.

finds a home in the A&M athletics museum at Kyle Field. The cup, however, isn't the only thing that has A&M fans glancing back to 1939.

That season and in that era, college football teams were graded by multiple polls and ratings organizations. Ten different groups, including the Associated Press, judged the 11-0 Aggies as the nation's best team in 1939. Cornell (8-0) was named No. 1 by two groups.

Southern California (8-0-2) was named the nation's top team by Frank Dickinson, a professor of economics at the University of Illinois who devised a points system for the purpose of picking a national champion. Dickinson gave up his system the following year.

Because of Dickinson's calculations that season, USC officials laid claim in the fall of 2004 to 1939 as one of its 11 national title seasons.

Ironically, in early 1940 promoters tried to match A&M and USC in an extra game to end any debate. The proceeds from the game were marked for a Finland war relief fund. Herbert Hoover, seven years removed from the White House, was said to have found the idea of a shootout "interesting." But the game never took place.

The 1939 Aggies figured they didn't need an extra game to establish their national superiority, anyway. They had a top ranking in the AP poll—and a shiny, handsome trophy proclaiming them Sugar Bowl champions.

Proof enough, they figured.

Now, from out of the dungeons of old Kyle Field, that sterling silver reminder of A&M football's most golden day is basking in the light of Aggieland once again.

> "MAN, BACK UP IN THERE YOU COULD HEAR THE PHANTOM OF THE OPERA."
>
> —R.C. Slocum on what it was like to stand deep in the bowels of historic Kyle Field

CHAPTER EIGHT

Hullabaloo Potluck

A few Texas A&M stories were so unique they didn't really fit in any other chapter in *More Tales From Aggieland*. Here are a few of those accounts that range from silly to stirring.

Gladiators on the Track

Chariots of Fire had just won an Oscar for best picture in 1981, the last time the Texas A&M men's track and field team had won a conference title. So the Aggies had plenty to celebrate in 2001 when the men earned their first league championship in 20 years.

"This is our *Gladiator*," said javelin winner Luke Marrs, referring to 2001's Oscar winner for best picture. "This is our Coliseum."

That year A&M played host to the conference track meet in College Station for the first time since 1990 and for the first time ever as a member of the Big 12 Conference. A defiant, can't-lose attitude permeated the Aggies like the sword of Russell Crowe's Maximus through a foe—especially because A&M's opponents had invaded Aggieland for the meet.

"I didn't want anybody to take the championship from me in my own backyard," said Aggie Jon Nance, who catapulted 18 feet to win the pole-vault competition.

"Some of these guys weren't even born in 1981," said Aggie coach Ted Nelson, who has been a part of the A&M program for nearly four decades.

Some members of Nelson's 1996 team that narrowly missed winning the final Southwest Conference championship attended the meet. The coach said he hugged them and told them he knew title didn't make up for such a close call.

"And they said, 'Yes it did, Coach,'" Nelson said.

FEBRUARY 14, 1998
BARONE ON THE HUNT

Texas A&M basketball coach Tony Barone said he's searching for a few good guys to fill out his basketball roster, now drained by injuries and academics. The 0-11 Aggies are scheduled to play Missouri this week with only eight players.

Barone said he'd like to get a couple of football players, but why stop there? There's a campus loaded with potential E. King Gills of the hardwood. Here are a few suggestions.

• Aggie center fielder Jason Tyner. Speed on the break. Would make a nice backcourt match with hustlin' Brian Barone.

• Tennis star Lisa Dingwall. Just the fiery spark-plug the Aggies need. Most of the hoopsters show little emotion, making fans think they don't care about losing. The excitable Dingwall yells on the court and once whacked her sister, Nancy, with her racket during a high school doubles match. In the state tournament. How's that for electrifying?

• The women's soccer team. Just wipe the slate clean and trot out any five of these players for the tip. At least this tight-knit bunch looks like it has fun playing the game—or playing cards. Or studying.

• All-America diver Mark Naftanel. Might add a touch of grace to the oft-disjointed goings on.

• Volleyball superstar Stacy "Sky" Sykora. A high-flyer with a gift for gab, Sykora already has lettered in volleyball, women's basketball, and track. The flashy, pretty Sykora may not score any points (although she probably would), but her addition at least would solve the Ags' attendance problems.

One problem: The university would need extra towel boys to wipe up after the slobbering students attending their first basketball game. Bonus: The Aggies' offering in any slam dunk competition.

• A handful of rec center regulars. They may not be six foot five, but some of those guys can shoot better than 30 percent from the three-point line. And sink a free throw.

• Swimmer Jennifer Guillory. One of the smartest Aggies to ever come down the pipe, maybe she could design an A&M offense where the team doesn't have to shoot.

• Billy Pickard, associate athletic director for facilities. He was there when G. Rollie White Coliseum opened, so let's shut the old barn's doors on a Pickard-led fast break. There might be some question about his eligibility, but if the Texas football team had an impostor—hey, it couldn't be any worse than what former coach Kermit Davis Jr. did in his reckless year here.

• All-America hurdler Larry Wade. Barone's players used to sprawl for the ball on defense. Now only his son does. Wade might have been more useful a couple of years ago.

• Golfer Jamie Hullett. Can sink it from 15 feet.

• Aggie linebacker Dat Nguyen. He can clear the lane with one swipe for a teammate's layup and then give all of the fellows—including the scrubs on the bench—credit for being good guys who without them wouldn't have made his good fortunes possible. Plus he can really hoop.

• Gary Kubiak. Mention his name for anything and make some Old Ags happy.

• "Voice of the Aggies" Dave South. If Barone says to (heck) with this (stuff) and becomes a candlestick maker—he once mentioned that as an option—South can make a Larry Dierker-like move from the broadcast booth to the sidelines. Plus, everyone knows we've got all the answers on press row.

Classy Goodbye

In a somewhat surreal yet mostly seamless transition, R.C. Slocum, A&M's all-time winningest football coach, said his gridiron goodbyes on a crisp mid-December night in 2002 before a packed ballroom at the 2002 Texas A&M Football Awards Banquet.

Before a slew of 2003 football prospects sprinkled among the crowd in the Zone Club of Kyle Field, Slocum recruited to the end, saying he'd had opportunities to coach at other places.

"But I never found a place better than Texas A&M," Slocum said. "That's why I'm here tonight. I plan on staying here and being here to watch you play. I always wanted a place where I could go and look a recruit in the eye and tell him, if you pick this school, you're making a great choice. And not have to have my fingers crossed when I said it."

Slocum told the prospects that with the addition of a sterling new football complex and other improvements underway on campus, "There's no better time in our history to be a football player than what's coming up right now."

Slocum's final pitch brought thunderous applause.

Alan Weddell, who coached linebackers under Slocum, profusely thanked the crowd for his five years spent at A&M.

"Some people come to A&M to become college coaches," said Weddell, who played football at Texas. "I got into college coaching to become an Aggie."

> "IF WE'VE GOT SOME ALUMNUS OR BOOSTER OUT THERE IN SOME OTHER FIELD OR ENDEAVOR THAT KNOWS MORE ABOUT OUR FOOTBALL TEAM AND WHAT WE SHOULD BE DOING, THEN WE'RE IN BIG, BIG TROUBLE."
>
> —*Football coach R.C. Slocum in 1996*

R.C. Slocum (back row, third from right) won more games than any A&M football coach in history.

Just Like the Bear

Paul "Bear" Bryant once gave an emotional speech to Texas A&M's Corps of Cadets shortly after his arrival from the University of Kentucky in 1954. On a cool March evening in 2003, the Corps—complete with the Aggie Band—joined recently hired coach Dennis Franchione and his football team following their first practice.

The Corps and band members, who also played "The Aggie War Hymn," joined forces with the football team and took a knee on the practice fields just south of Kyle Field to hear a short speech from Franchione.

There were plenty of "whoops" all around and even a "Beat the hell outta Iraq!" cheer led by A&M's yell leaders during the unrehearsed get-together. America's war with Iraq had just begun.

Coach Fran

Catch Texas A&M football coach Dennis Franchione with a hammer in his hand, the family joke goes, and you'd better call 911.

Paul "Bear" Bryant delivered a rousing speech at The Grove shortly after his arrival from Kentucky in 1954.

"I have no talent in building anything," Franchione said with a chuckle, "other than a team."

Pete and Theda Franchione once taught their son plenty about building—mostly a work ethic—even if the boy didn't exactly take to all of the details. But, oh, did Pete especially work the youngster, figuring it was the best way to introduce the kid to higher education.

The son, looking back on those formative years in Kansas, considers those countless hours of blue-collar, teenaged tedium just one long college entrance exam.

"My mom and dad weren't college-educated, and I'm not sure that my dad was high-school educated," Franchione said. "But the one thing they made sure I did was work for everything. I had some miserable, tough jobs, by Dad's design. He wanted me to go to college and get an education.

"I hung insulation. I hauled hay from early in the morning until late at night. I got all of the grunt jobs. And it became very vivid to me that I didn't want to do those kinds of things for a living."

In 1978, Kansas State coach Jim Dickey Sr. hired the ambitious, bright young man who'd already made three high school pit stops in his quest to enter the college ranks. Dickey hired Franchione as an assistant for $13,000 a year, a move the head coach soon deemed invaluable.

"Recruiting is such an important part of coaching in college, and you knew if he was in a recruit's home we had a 90 percent chance of getting the guy," Dickey said. "People just like him. He's charismatic and sincere, and the more you're around him, the more you like him."

Dickey enjoys telling how he and Franchione once pulled up in front of a recruit's house, with a spry Franchione brand new to the job but still offering a little friendly advice to his boss.

"Coach, this kid really likes me, and if he likes you, we've got him," an optimistic but cautious Franchione told Dickey. "If you don't mess it up, we've got him."

"What do you mean, putting it on me?" a wide-eyed Dickey responded, shaking his head but immediately recognizing a focus that would lead to big things for the youngster from Girard, Kansas.

Jasper Proud

Red Bryant, then barely a teenager, knocked on James Byrd's door at the Pine View Apartments in Bryant's hometown of Jasper that spring day in 1998. Then, a naughty but playful Bryant got ready to flee the scene.

"We'd run around the apartments, knocking on people's doors and being mischievous," recalled Bryant, a defensive tackle for Texas A&M.

But before Bryant could vacate Byrd's doorstep, Byrd opened the door. He grinned at Bryant and his sister, Anna.

"I was thirsty, so I asked Mr. Byrd for a glass of water," Bryant said. "He gave me a 7-Up. I'll always remember his kindness. Here I was, being mischievous, and he still gave me that glass of 7-Up."

That June, three white supremacists dragged Byrd, a black man, to his death—a racially motivated murder that drew worldwide attention and brought scorn on the small town of Jasper.

"I was scared right after that happened," Bryant said. "I slept in my mom's bed when I first heard about it. It was a scary time."

Bryant, who signed with the Aggies in 2003, said it's unfair that what happened in Jasper six years ago should scar his hometown forever.

Dennis Franchione has adopted the goalpost lean and look that Bear Bryant made famous before him.

"If God sees fit, and I live to be old, I'd love to go back and live there," Bryant said. "We need to show that the community as a whole is better than what people's perception is."

SECTION II

On the Beat

CHAPTER NINE

Dave South's Greatest Bits

Dave South, Texas A&M's associate athletic director, possesses one of the most distinct voices in college athletics and is truly the Voice of the Aggies—which he's been since 1985. This chapter recounts some of South's favorite, funnier, and sometimes plain nutty moments in two decades of broadcasting Aggie athletics.

Getting Started

At the end of the 1984 season Dave South had made the decision to leave the football broadcast booth while working for the Southwest Conference radio network and concentrate on his broadcast management position.

In the spring of 1985 the late Ralph Carpenter, then an assistant athletic director at Texas A&M, called to say that the fellow who was going to do the football games for the Aggies that season had said he was leaving the state. Carpenter wanted to know if South would consider filling in for one year and then they could find someone else in 1986.

Well, South had always had a strong feeling about Texas A&M and what the university stood for. His wife's father was class of 1941. His

Dave South has served as the Voice of the Aggies for two decades.

fifth-grade homeroom teacher was Mary Todd. Her husband was the legendary Dick Todd, who played at A&M in the late 1930s. Dick Todd used to come to the school where she taught and talk about Texas A&M and play football with the boys.

So South had some Aggie background. He said he'd do it.

That August, when two-a-days started, South made arrangements to come down for a Saturday scrimmage at Kyle Field. He had never met coach Jackie Sherrill and knew very little about him.

Late in the scrimmage that day one of the players had moved to the bench and taken off his jersey and his shoulder pads, and was talking to a *Bryan-College Station Eagle* sportswriter, who was taking notes and obviously doing a story for his paper.

The next thing everyone knew, Sherrill was yelling loud enough for everyone in the stadium to hear him and barking for the sports information director. The coach was upset about the sportswriter being on the bench and doing the interview.

"Maybe this isn't such a good idea after all," South thought.

He couldn't recall in 25 years of being around athletics, at any level, hearing someone get screamed at like that in public. First thing South knew, Carpenter had moved in behind him in the stands at Kyle. Carpenter was talking a mile a minute.

"Now, Dave, don't let that bother you—he's just having a bad day," Carpenter said. "He really is a good guy; he'll never talk to you like that. You'll get along great."

The chamber of commerce would have loved his speech. South looked around and raised his eyebrows.

"Okay," he said, "I'll take your word on it."

Sherrill couldn't have been nicer to South over the next four seasons. They became very good friends. And South's one-year commitment to Texas A&M has turned into more than 20 years.

Tiger Stadium

Texas A&M was playing at LSU's Tiger Stadium in 1988, and that season the Aggie broadcast team was doing a fan-in-the-stand feature for each broadcast. When A&M played at Kyle Field, South went out into the stands with a wireless microphone and interviewed people sitting in the third deck.

On the road he had to go to the area where A&M's fans had tickets. Tiger Stadium visiting fans sit in the corner of the end zone on the other side of the stadium from the press box, so South had a long way to go. He carried his recorder and wearing an Aggie shirt, found the father of A&M offensive lineman Jerry Fontenot.

The Fontenots were from Louisiana, so they understood the mentality of some Tiger fans. South asked Fontenot if he could give him about three minutes on tape. As they began talking, someone with slurred speech came up behind South, so close that he could smell alcohol on his breath, and started cussing South with any and all words.

Fontenot wasn't fazed by any of this. South kept asking questions and never looked around at the guy. The cusser went on for about another 30 seconds, and then it sounded like he choked on his words, and the cussing stopped.

When South finished the interview, he asked Fontenot what had happened to the guy, and Fontenot said that a state trooper had grabbed him around the neck and lugged him away.

After the game, coach Jackie Sherrill and South did a long postgame show, which didn't allow the two to get on the bus with the team. They were to be given a ride in a police car, which turned out to be a highway patrol car. South went ahead of Sherrill and got in the front seat and told the trooper the coach would join them in a few minutes.

"Were you interviewing one of the Aggie fans before the game?" the trooper asked.

South nodded.

"What did you think about the guy who was cussing you?" he asked.

South's eyes widened a bit.

"Were you the one who hauled him off?" he asked.

"Yes," the trooper said, "I was hoping he'd hit you."

South told him he didn't think that was a proper thing for a law enforcement officer to say.

"Don't get me wrong," the trooper said, waving his hands. "If he had hit you, I could have hit him. I can't stand that guy. After he left he went over and started messing with one of your Aggie Band boys. I was hoping he would hit a band guy. I can't tell you how much I want to hit that guy."

West Coast Trip

Without naming names, the baseball team had gone to California for a tournament some years back. The players had some free time to go to a mall to eat and walk around. One of the official members of the traveling party had gone into a sporting goods store to look at some shorts.

He found a pair he liked, so he strolled into the dressing room, took off his pants, and was about to put on the shorts. He heard a knock and went to the door, only to find no one there. The knock had actually come from behind him.

He turned around and realized at that moment that he had not walked into the dressing room, but into the store's display window. The knock was against the front window—and there were some of the baseball players laughing their heads off.

Dave and Dave

Dave Elmendorf was a football All-American, baseball All-American, and academic All-American at Texas A&M. He played nine years in the NFL and became an All-Pro for the Los Angeles Rams. Elmendorf continues to be a great ambassador for his university.

Elmendorf lettered for the Aggies from 1968 to 1970 and played in some lean seasons with not a lot of football victories.

Fast-forward to 1991. Elmendorf and South were sitting in a hotel lobby in Baton Rouge, Louisiana, where the Aggies were to play Louisiana State later that night. They were simply watching people walk by and talking with some about the upcoming game.

An older gentleman, using a cane to walk, started heading their way. It became apparent he was heading straight toward South, who stood up and extended his hand.

"I'm Dave South," he said.

"I know who you are," he said. "I've been wanting to meet you."

The gentleman added that he listened to the games when he couldn't attend and was looking forward to the contest that night. South suddenly realized he hadn't introduced the old man to Elmendorf.

Elmendorf stood up and offered his hand. The Old Ag glanced at him and turned and said to South, "I know who he is. He dropped the punt in the Michigan game."

That had happened in 1970. The old-timer refused to shake Elmendorf's hand and turned and walked away as fast as his cane and gait would allow. Some people just can't let go.

Tossed from a Game

Officials in the Southwest Conference had been having a bad year in 1993. Leading into the SWC basketball tournament that season in Dallas, a journalist from the *Houston Post* had written a story on the officiating. The coaches, who remained anonymous in the article, all pretty much said the same thing: The refereeing had hit an all-time low.

In the first half of the game between Texas A&M and Houston, the Aggies had more fouls than the Cougars. South pointed that out. The second half started out the same way. With less than 10 minutes remaining, the game was in a timeout and South was in a commercial break and had his headset down around his neck and was sipping on a cola.

He thought about what was going on out on the floor. Normally when there is a three-man crew, one official places himself on the baseline to observe the bench of Team A. The second official goes to the other baseline to observe Team B. The third official is to stand at midcourt to watch for the signal that the timeout is over.

But the third official had placed himself on the free-throw line with his back to the timekeeper and was standing directly in front of South, who was located across from the A&M bench on the second row of press tables.

South looked away at the Houston bench and then looked back at the official. The ref was still standing there. South smiled, toasted him with his cup, and raised his right hand to his throat to indicate that he and his officials had choked.

The official turned to his right and walked to the baseline, got a security guard, came back to South's side of the floor, and began screaming that he had thrown South out of the game and for him to get up, leave the sidelines, and not come back.

Because the game was practically over—Houston had a big lead—many of the media members followed South out. When they were under the stands, South asked that someone go and get A&M's athletic director, John David Crow. South didn't talk to the media—only to Crow. Crow stood up for South and said he'd talk to the media.

Not only was South taken off the floor, the security guard was about to take him out of the arena. South was on his way to the street. When they got to the front door, South stopped and asked that they radio someone from the SWC to listen to what he had to say.

Colin Killian, A&M's basketball sports information director, had been left to finish the broadcast, but he couldn't do the postgame show due to postgame press conference needs. South was able to convince the league official that once the game was over, he had the right to return to the floor and do his postgame show. The security guard took him down to floor level, where they were going to lock him in a room.

As they were walking by the tunnel back to the floor, Texas coach Tom Penders walked over to South, hugged him, and whispered in his ear, "You're my new hero."

The official in question was one of the referees who had come under fire in the *Houston Post* story. One of the SWC coaches said that he would just as soon have a dog call his game as that referee. The rules clearly state that to be kicked out of a game one has to be interfering with the play of the game. In South's case it was a timeout—there was no play on the floor.

South believes he was the straw that broke the camel's back. The head of officials was dismissed along with some 20 to 25 of his people after that season. The league and the calls got much better the next season, and South had his 15 seconds of fame.

He was on ESPN's *SportsCenter,* and in most newspapers around the country, and the comic strip "Tank McNamara" did a week on the incident. To this day it will pop up once or twice a year on some sports calendar pad that people use at work. The "Tank" folks sent South the original artwork and autographed it. He framed it and hung it in the office at home.

Would he do it all over again? No way!

Pizza in the Dugout

Baseball players have too much time on their hands. When pitcher Jeff Granger was in Aggieland in the early 1990s, he would take a radio and headset to the bullpen (when he wasn't scheduled to pitch) and listen to the broadcast of the game.

Back in the late 1980s, though, the broadcast had a contest that when an Aggie hit a home run, the first, second, or third caller to the radio station got a free pizza delivered. The promotion was a big hit with the fans. Terry Taylor, one of A&M's infielders, would make a mad dash into the locker room, grab the trainers' phone, and try to win the pizza.

South often wondered what coach Mark Johnson would've done if the pizza delivery guy had walked into the dugout at Olsen and tried to deliver the pizza to Taylor.

The Marines in Georgia

A&M basketball had gone to Savannah, Georgia, for a game against Georgia Southern in 1996. It's rare that the Aggies go anywhere where they don't have A&M fans show up to support the team.

That night there was a group of Aggies with their wives and families. If time allows, South tries to go up into the stands and visit with the A&M faithful and in some cases give the folks a few media guides.

Each one of these four guys was wearing a high and tight haircut. They were all Aggies and Marine Corps pilots stationed at a nearby base. They'd heard about the game and wanted to see the team. South had a nice visit with them and went back to the broadcast table.

That night two guys in their mid- to late 20s showed up wearing Longhorn shirts and caps. When the A&M team ran out on the floor, the two fellows were standing on the baseline screaming, "Hook 'em, Horns!" and a few other negative comments about A&M. They stayed there until the game started.

Each time there was a timeout they stood right behind A&M's bench and yelled as loud as they could—the same ol' stuff. After the second timeout, Aggie coach Tony Barone started moving the team out on the floor to get away from them.

The obnoxious fellows continued to stand on the sideline and to yell louder—making complete fools of themselves.

The game ended, and South was off the air and putting his equipment up, and two of the Marines came back across the floor from one of the corner doors leading out of the building. They were moving really fast. South thanked them for coming, and they waved, grabbed their families, hurried up the steps, and exited at the lower concourse.

The team loaded onto the bus, and as the bus drove around the other side of the arena, there was an ambulance with its back doors open. On a stretcher, in the back, was one of the Texas fans—and the other fan was standing outside giving a report to the police.

The team started laughing—and South knew then why the two Marines were in such a hurry. One of them had punched the guy, to let him know his behavior wasn't acceptable in Georgia with the USMC—and a couple of Aggie Marines.

"WE'RE PLAYING."

—Aggie fan Clifford George's explanation on why he and buddy James Storrs hopped in a car and drove 933 miles and 13 straight hours to see A&M play in the 1999 College World Series in Omaha, Nebraska

---

A "Glamorous" Job

South always tell these stories when someone says, "You have such a glamorous job!":

Kansas State was in the process of renovating its baseball field in 1999. The Wildcats were playing all of their "home" games on the road that season and scheduled A&M for St. Joseph, Missouri. Aggie head coach Mark Johnson had called some folks to get a report on the stadium. The feedback? It was as bad as a gravel pit.

Coach spent time with the team at the hotel before the Friday game telling the players, "Don't let it get to you when you get a bad hop or when you lose the ball because of poor lighting."

It was worse than anyone imagined. The thing was built in the 1930s, and the legendary Yogi Berra had played his minor league baseball at this place. The lights were mounted on tripod towers and were located inside the fence—and there was chain-link fencing around the towers.

If the ball went inside that fence, it was a ground-rule double. The stands were wood, and bench-type seating was all that was available. It was cold, and the crowd would be less than 100 all three days.

Here's South's part of the story: The press box was on the roof above the stands. Broadcasters walked to the top of the stands, and there was a ladder leading up to a trap door that then led to the edge of the roof, where the press box had been built.

South carries a case that weighs about 75 pounds, with all of the radio equipment. Chuck Glenewinkel, A&M's baseball sports information director, climbed to the top of the ladder, then laid down on the roof and reached down to grab the radio case, and pulled as South pushed.

The coaches and the team stopped what they were doing to watch Glenewinkel and South work to get this stuff up the ladder. Following the radio equipment were the briefcases. To the press box they went.

The visiting broadcast booth had not been used in years. There was an air conditioner in the chair where South was supposed to sit for the game. Glenewinkel and South had to pick it up and take it back out on the roof, where they left it. For all they know, it might still be there.

Their view of the game was from the edge of the roof, looking straight down on home plate. If someone suffered from a fear of heights, he would have been in serious trouble. Because there was no lock on the press box, they had to reverse the process at the end of the game with the equipment, and then do the same thing on Saturday and Sunday.

Anyone who has covered a game for radio or a newspaper can offer up stories like these. There have been times when South was in a room with the other team's radio crew, the press box personnel, and the writers. There was so much talk going on the folks back home couldn't understand what he was saying into the microphone.

South remembers turning on the heater in a major college football press box early in the fall. The next thing they knew, the whole booth was full of yellow jackets. The little fellows had built a nest under the heater, and he'd woken them up.

Everyone but the engineer, color guy, and South left. A sports information department member came in with wasp spray, while they were on the air, and killed them all. It would have been a tape to listen to if South had gotten stung on a big play.

There was another college baseball press box that was located on top of the concession stand, and by the end of the game the smoke from the hot dogs and hamburgers was so strong it made South's eyes water.

Yet another major college baseball venue put South in a press box that looked like a pasture feed barn for cattle—only the feed barn would have been bigger. Every time someone changed anything on the scoreboard (balls, strikes, outs, hits, runs, errors) it put a loud buzz on his equipment—and on the radios back home in Bryan–College Station.

South remembers going to Ohio Stadium for a SWC network broadcast and the airline lost the equipment. The engineer went all over Columbus, Ohio, that Friday afternoon. He begged and borrowed enough to get the radio crew on the air.

No fancy headsets, not even close. South had a microphone designed for a table stand, but they didn't have a stand. They took a clothes hanger and wired it around his neck. South often wondered what the folks in Columbus thought about that high-tech crew from Texas.

As South looks back on all of these stories—and many more—he can laugh about them, but he laughs harder when someone says, "What a glamorous job!"

The Game at Notre Dame

In 2000, the football team traveled to Notre Dame to play the Fighting Irish. South has a very close friend—let's call him Charles—who will do anything to help. South had asked him to be in the radio booth at Notre Dame to serve as a runner between the broadcast booth and the sports information folks in the press box.

That day in South Bend, Indiana, turned out to be one of the hottest days in years for that part of the country. There is no air conditioning in the Notre Dame press box, because they usually don't need it—but they did that day.   South made a comment about how hot it was. The sun was coming right in on the crew, and there was no breeze.

Within a few minutes some workers walked in pushing a fan that looked like it had been a prop on a plane. South asked what they were doing, and they said some guy asked to find a large fan and take it to the visiting radio booth. Just then Charles walked in.

"Good," he said, "you brought the fan."

South told Charles that if they turned that fan on it would blow everyone out of the booth and down into the stands—and certainly would interfere with the microphones for the broadcast.

The next five or 10 minutes passed with little happening, then the same workers began bringing in tables and chairs. The Notre Dame booth was a big one, and suddenly they had enough tables and chairs to hold a tailgate party for about 30 people.

South asked what was going on, and the workers patiently said the same guy who'd asked for the fan had requested the tables and chairs. Charles walked in and said, "Good, you brought the tables and chairs."

"Charles, what are you doing?" South asked.

"Well, Dave, you need some workspace to get ready for the broadcast, the engineer needs space for the equipment, and we'll want to eat in here," he calmly responded.

South settled on one table and five chairs. The next thing South knew Charles strolled in with media guides, multiple A&M and Notre Dame game notes, game programs, and enough roster cards for everyone in the press box. South explained to Charles that he and Dave Elmendorf had all of those things mailed to them earlier in the week and that Charles could take them all back.

South really likes the guy and would never say anything to hurt his feelings, but he was getting close. Then, once they got on the air, during every commercial break in the pregame show he would come up behind South and ask about three or four questions.

The crew was finally down to the last break before the teams kicked off. There was a tap on South's right shoulder. He put both his arms above his head, turned his palms to face the back of the room, and gave a violent motion with his palms, hands, and arms to move back and leave him alone. Then he looked to his right at Elmendorf and at the stat person, and they had wide-eyed, open-mouthed expressions. South turned expecting to look at Charles—only it wasn't Charles. It was A&M's athletic director and South's boss, Wally Groff.

Now with just under 30 seconds until South started talking, he ran to Groff before he left the room to tell him he was sorry, please forgive him, and let him keep his job.

Needless to say it was not a comfortable first quarter in the broadcast booth.

Foot in Mouth

One of South's friends at Texas A&M is Billy Pickard, the university's longtime director of athletic facilities. The two talk, play golf, and share a lot of stories. Pickard has a reputation for telling people exactly how he feels. South doesn't always agree—but he likes knowing how Pickard feels.

A&M was playing in a Cotton Bowl in the early 1990s. The team was staying at the Hyatt on the edge of downtown Dallas. There's a nice breakfast area on the second level of the hotel, and South was sitting at a table next to Wally and Patty Groff. Pickard came in and talked to Wally for a few minutes, looked at South, and without saying a word walked away.

Some 30 minutes later South saw Pickard again, this time with his wife, Linda, and walked over to him and asked if he was upset with about something. He said no.

"Well, you came over to Wally's table and talked to him, and you looked at me and walked away without saying a word," South said.

"You had that goofy-looking guy sitting with you with the purple hair, wild clothes, and braids, and I didn't want to bother you," he replied. "Who was that idiot?"

"My youngest son," South said.

The two have stayed good friends, but South will bring that one up to Pickard from time to time.

Trip to San Angelo

When Tony Barone was at A&M (from 1991 to 1998), South would often travel with him when Barone was asked to speak at an A&M club somewhere in the state. His very first trip was to San Angelo, Texas. South had been there a number of times and really enjoyed the hospitality and good people in West Texas.

South assured Barone that he would have a great time. They left College Station early in the morning and drove to San Angelo. South kept telling Barone what a great time he was going to have.

They hadn't been at the meeting more than five minutes when a guy came up and asked, "Coach, why are all basketball coaches short, fat Italians?"

South received a glance and glare from Barone and then held his breath for what was about to be said.

Barone finally answered, "Because we're good at answering stupid questions."

CHAPTER TEN

A Sports Reporter's Delight

There's a reason I chose to return to Aggieland to cover Texas A&M—it's a good place to be and an exciting, dynamic environment in which to work. The folks below agree. I asked some of the sports reporters who've covered the Aggies over the decades to recount some of their favorite or more memorable tales.

Ride of a Lifetime

Flying into Fayetteville, Arkansas, was no joyride any time in the 1970s, because the plane had to come in over a mountain, and it always seemed like the wreckage of some ill-fated flight was sitting beside the runway. But one trip in the mid-1970s will live forever in infamy.

Jim Butler—a movie critic for *The Bryan-College Station Eagle* and A&M Class of 1964—served as assistant sports information director for Texas A&M athletics, and basketball was one of his responsibilities, so he traveled with the team. On this particular frosty February morning, coach Shelby Metcalf and the Aggie basketball team arrived at Easterwood Airport to board a charter flight to Fayetteville. The plane was an old DC-3 with "Baja Airlines" written on the side. In the window of the cockpit was a sign: For Sale.

As the plane was revving its engines preparing for takeoff, one of the engines caught on fire. Butler and the rest of the passengers had to get off the plane and wait for the problem to be fixed. Believe it or not, they got back on that same plane.

The flight was supposed to be nonstop to Fayetteville, but after it had been in the air for just a few minutes, the pilot came on the intercom and said that the plane had lost oil pressure and that they were going to have to land in Dallas. The plane's heater was out, so everyone was freezing. As the plane sputtered into Dallas, it was flying so low that the passengers had to look up at the skyscrapers.

When the plane landed, everyone rushed off of it and immediately threw up on the runway.

Gracious in Defeat

Two of the more unusual incidents Robert Cessna, the current executive sports editor for *The Bryan-College Station Eagle*, experienced covering A&M football dealt with people's emotions.

Emory Bellard was the head coach when Cessna first came to B–CS in the mid-1970s. Bellard was a well-respected man, very professional.

He had some great teams, elevating the program, but the fans wanted more. A&M started the 1978 season with four victories, outscoring the opposition 170-21. A&M was in the top 10 and had visions of a national championship. But after getting bounced at Houston (33-0), the Aggies came home and lost to Baylor (24-6).

It was a crushing loss. Speculation on Bellard's job heightened during the second half. A&M had stumbled in 1977, losing three of its last five games—to Arkansas, Texas, and Southern Cal. Some said this might be the last straw, that this would be his last year.

Fans had grown tired of the Wishbone offense. It was great when A&M was ahead, but when the Aggies fell behind, it didn't have a chance. Cessna was to write the locker-room story after the Baylor game. In those days reporters walked into the locker room and watched the players and coaches head into and out of the showers. They were interviewed as they dressed or undressed.

Someone from the athletic department usually tried to help, but reporters were basically on their own. Those actually were the good old

Coach Emory Bellard encourages star running back Curtis Dickey, who also was a standout track athlete.

days. Scribes heard anything and everything in that setting. Well, no one could find Bellard. Hundreds of people—but no Bellard.

One after one, the writers gave up and headed out. Finally, Bellard emerged. He had a towel wrapped around him. He was solemn, much like a heavyweight boxer who had lost his one and only championship fight.

Cessna felt his pain. It was Cessna, a rookie reporter from the school newspaper, and one other writer who were left to interview Bellard. It was easily Cessna's toughest assignment yet. What do you say in such a situation?

Cessna started with a simple question—Did Baylor do anything different?—and so forth. A red-eyed Bellard graciously answered all of Cessna's questions. The following Monday, Bellard resigned.

The Big Lift

Eric Dickerson was one of the greatest high school running backs in the history of the state. Before the Sealy native signed with SMU after winning state in 1979, he made a recruiting trip to Texas A&M.

He attended a basketball game against Houston. Robert Cessna decided to write a story on Dickerson's trip. He waited until halftime and walked over to Dickerson, who was being shown around campus by All-American Jacob Green.

Cessna wasn't one of Green's favorite reporters, because he'd picked the Aggies to lose several games—they had lost five games that previous season. As Cessna introduced himself, Dickerson started shaking his head.

"I don't want to talk to any more reporters," he said.

"You especially don't want to talk to him," Green added.

Before Cessna could ask another question, he felt two hands planted firmly on his shoulders, lifting him up. It was head coach Tom Wilson.

Wilson said that Cessna could not talk to Dickerson. That was one of the agreements he had with Dickerson to get him to visit. Wilson also said that was an agreement that he made with Cessna's boss, as he escorted the young writer from the gym.

Cessna was hot. Several writers asked him what had happened. He went back to the office and got ready to pound out a column about Wilson grabbing and lifting him. However, the sports editor and managing editor told Cessna he was trying to make something out of nothing. They wouldn't allow the commentary to run.

That grabbing might have been okay in 1980, but can anyone imagine that happening today? Cessna was hot at Wilson, but not long after that, the coach apologized. The two actually had a great relationship after that, much better than before the incident.

Cessna followed Wilson's career to Palestine and Corsicana high schools, often talking to him during recruiting. In retrospect, Wilson was under a lot of pressure in 1980, and if he had gotten Dickerson, who knows what might have happened with the program? If Cessna had been able to write his column, well, Wilson probably would've never talked to him again.

Caught by the Shortstop

It was spring of 1980, before the Rice and Texas A&M baseball teams had become the national forces they are today. On a forgotten afternoon in Houston, at the old Owl stadium, the visiting radio announcers were set up on a porch-type platform of sorts behind home plate and in the middle of the stands.

Ernie Moore, the Aggies' veteran play-by-play man, was calling the action alongside Jon Heidtke, now general manager of Fox Sports Southwest in Dallas, and Richard Oliver, now a sports columnist for the *San Antonio Express-News*. Heidtke and Oliver were both student broadcast majors.

In a season that had included an uncomfortable number of errors on the field for the Aggies, a few miscues had been made behind the microphone, as well. Earlier in the year, after Oliver had noted that host A&M had collected a dozen hits in a game, Heidtke had responded, "Even the Beatles didn't have that many hits," as press-box listeners collectively groaned.

The response was markedly different in Houston when an Aggie batter stepped to the plate with Moore calling the action. The pitch came, the batter swung, the ball was struck.

"There's a long drive!" Moore hollered. Then, a pause for a heartbeat. "Caught," he added, sheepishly, "by the shortstop."

Around the makeshift platform, the guffaws from the legendarily ribald Rice fans rained down for the remainder of the game. With each followup swing by any batter, someone would bark out his own call.

"There's a long drive!" the fan would yell.

Even today, the answer brings a smile: "Caught by the shortstop."

12th Man Scoop

Jackie Sherrill arrived in Aggieland in 1982 with a record-breaking contract and a reputation as something of a snake-oil salesman. Back East, in places like Pittsburgh, Sherrill's previous stop, a suitcase and a good sales pitch are still considered trademarks of an innovative fellow who knows how to duck and dodge, whether the projectile be a fast taxi or, in Sherrill's case, a brick from the NCAA.

Having been born in Philadelphia and having studied the finer points of Sherrill's satiny bull for a year, Al Carter, now a deputy sports editor for the *San Antonio Express-News*, put his own salesman skills to the test one lazy afternoon in August 1983, Carter's second year of 18 years on the beat and Sherrill's second of seven as head coach.

The days were hot and long, and short of good preseason story topics. Sherrill and Carter, then with the *Houston Chronicle*, met in his office on the ninth floor of Rudder Tower and with the late-day sun radiating through the plate glass, exchanged small talk in mutual anticipation that his ego and Carter's access to the *Chronicle* sports page might lead to something interesting—something of benefit to both. And it did.

But only after Carter's Henry Hill meshed with Sherrill's Elmer Gantry. While Sherrill thumped on the bible of Texas A&M football, Carter played trombone to the beat. It made for hype and harmony on the front page of the next day's *Chronicle*.

Casually, cunningly, Sherrill mentioned that he had an idea for a new tradition at A&M involving the football team, one that would send the student body to bouncing whoops off Jupiter and (what he didn't say) would prompt full forgiveness from the faithful for Sherrill's 5-6 debut season in 1982. Sherrill said he would be glad to tell Carter all about it—in a few days.

"Tell me about what?" Carter said.

"I can't tell you right now."

"Why?"

"I just can't. There's someone I have to discuss it with first."

"Discuss what? With whom?"

"I can't go into it now. But when I announce it, you're going to love it. It's going to be big news!"

Being a reporter, big news was one of Carter's turn-ons.

"If you want it to be big news," Carter said, "you need to tell me what it is. That way I can discuss it with my editors, and if it's really something cool, we can do something really special with it. Maybe put it on the front page. Maybe a big photo. Something fancy. Something to really get people's attention."

Sherrill paused. His eyes got wide. He seemed to purr, like a Siamese cat, sitting in the sun on a favorite pillow. Then, just as suddenly, his head sagged.

"There's a problem with that," he said, feigning despair. "I've promised the story to another reporter."

"What other reporter?" Carter said.

"Ivy McLemore."

McLemore was Carter's competition at the *Houston Post*. McLemore had been to College Station a few days before, and Sherrill had told him all about his plan. But he asked McLemore to wait and not write it up until after he had announced it to the group it was going to impact most, his target audience. Having confessed that much, he told Carter his plan.

Sherrill was going to create a special unit of walk-on players to handle kickoff duties for his team. It was going to be Sherrill's attempt to bring the tradition of the 12th Man to life. Real students—in reality, former high-school players who were just below Division I caliber—would be given real uniforms and would play in real games as 12th Man members of the kickoff team. What Sherrill said next made the whole thing irresistible.

The participants on his new 12th Man unit would all come from the A&M Corps of Cadets.

Carter was stunned. Sherrill's 12th Man idea would be to Aggie culture what the Marshall Plan was to Europe, what beer is to fraternities. The idea that maniacal members of the Corps might be unleashed on the pumped and pampered icons of the Southwest Conference was carnival fare, akin to Parisian market maids storming the Buttercrust plant. Carter wasn't leaving Rudder without the story.

"I can get this on the front page of the *Chronicle* tomorrow morning," Carter blurted out.

Sherrill, Carter could tell, was beginning to construct a mockup of that front page in his mind. Carter began to wonder if his editor would deliver what he had just promised.

Sherrill struck next.

"You know," he said in a tantalizing voice, "I'm on my way over to the Corps dining hall right now. I'm going to make the announcement at dinner. And I guess there's nothing I can do to keep you from showing up and listening."

"So I can have the story, right? You'll talk to me about it, for the record?" Carter said.

"I don't know," said Sherrill, suddenly playing coy again. "I really promised this story to Ivy. I'm not sure I can break my promise."

"I'm here—Ivy's not," Carter said firmly. "I think I deserve something for being in the right place at the right time."

Carter's trump card. Sherrill, who lifted himself from humble origins with guile and a great sense of timing, agreed. He rose from his chair and headed for the door.

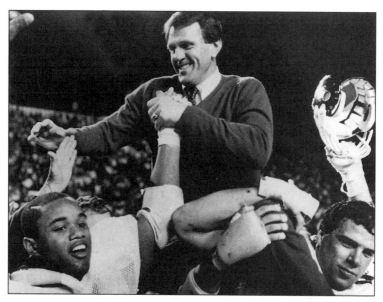

Jackie Sherrill shoved the A&M football team to prominence in the mid-1980s.

"I'll just have to tell Ivy he needs to come up here and see us more often," he said.

Carter walked with Sherrill to the dining hall and stood in the wings while the head football coach at Texas A&M used a microphone to announce that he was going to enlist members of the Corps to suit up and play on Saturdays at Kyle Field. The hall went spasmodic with every kind of exaltation ever devised by either man or beast.

Carter's editor loved it. The story, accompanied by a photo of the statue of original 12th Man E. King Gill, dominated the top half of the front page of the sports section the next morning. Sherrill was delighted. A&M fans were delighted. The 12th Man walk-on program, modified, lives on a generation later.

McLemore, although chagrined, never held it against Carter. Seven years later, after McLemore become sports editor of the *Post*, he hired Carter away from the *Chronicle*.

Sherrill resigned after the 1988 season, with the NCAA doing vulture loops around Rudder. The end came about three months after Carter wrote a column for the *Chronicle* in which he offered the opinion that Sherrill should quit or be fired. In 35 years of journalism Sherrill remains the only person about whom Carter ever made such a comment. Carter took a stab at one last meeting with Sherrill in his Rudder office.

With the end only hours away, Carter sat on a couch in the lobby with two other sportswriters. All of them wanted to interview the embattled boss. Sherrill's secretary emerged with her right index finger raised.

"Coach Sherrill will talk to you and he'll talk to you," she said, pointing at Carter's colleagues. Carter was the last to be fingered.

"He will not talk to you."

It's not every day that every good salesman can get his foot in every door.

The Quotable Coach

Until recently, covering Texas A&M basketball was always an adventure—and seldom in a good way. In 22 years, there have been five different coaches. But only one, Shelby Metcalf, provided consistent entertainment. "The Good Doctor" was always quick with a quip. He had to have a sense of humor to coach basketball at A&M for 27 seasons.

One night in Austin while Chip Howard, now a host for *Sports Talk* on KZNE radio, was preparing to call a game against the Longhorns, Metcalf came up to Howard's wife, who was sitting next to him, and told her that his assistant coach was a ventriloquist. The Howards looked a little puzzled, but Metcalf explained, "If you think you hear me cussin' during the game, it's my assistant. He can throw his voice."

Everyone's a Critic

There was a reason Chip Howard only lasted three years calling games for basketball coach Shelby Metcalf. His wife and daughter would faithfully listen to each word Howard said and would hand him a list of "negative comments" as he walked in the door after each game.

They particularly didn't like what Howard thought was a "throwaway" line used during a game against Bob Knight's Indiana Hoosiers at the Indiana Classic in Bloomington in 1983. In those days Knight wore those garish plaid jackets.

But in the opening game against the Aggies, Knight was dressed in a regular sport coat. Howard said he guessed Knight was saving the plaid jacket for the final the next night. Metcalf and the Aggies lost to the

Hoosiers 73-48. By the way, Indiana had a pretty good freshman guard by the name of Steve Alford.

Wear of the Road

Shelby Metcalf's coaching nemesis was Eddie Sutton. He had a hard time beating Sutton's Razorbacks (as did most other teams in the old Southwest Conference). Apparently, Metcalf tried just about everything when the team had to travel to Fayetteville, including different wardrobes and staying in different hotels during their trips to the Ozarks.

When told of the superstitious ways of the coach by one of his assistants, Chip Howard replied that if he stayed in a different hotel and wore different clothes every trip while trying to get a win, he was going to run out of clothes and hotel rooms.

MARCH 9, 1996
BEMOANING THE DEMISE OF SWC BASKETBALL

DALLAS – Today the curtains drop on Southwest Conference basketball forever, but league beat reporters will tell you it lost its main character more than 10 years ago when former Arkansas coach Eddie Sutton split for Kentucky.

His old school followed suit in 1991 when it bolted for the Southeastern Conference.

"Since Arkansas left, the conference has been dead," says WTAW Radio's Chip Howard, a longtime voice in Aggieland. "Texas Tech is the closest thing to what Arkansas used to have, but you'd have to double their number of fans."

Reporters both shake their heads and grin at Sutton's means of doing things—some of which make Dallas Cowboy owner Jerry Jones seem laissez-faire.

"It was the most absurd thing I've ever seen in sports," says Al Carter, *The Dallas Morning News* beat writer for Texas A&M, of an incident at the 1982 SWC Classic at Reunion Arena.

Arkansas was battling Houston in the finals, and Sutton carried on a conversation with then-SWC head of officials Bob Prewitt—while the teams ran up and down the court. At that time, coaches could get two technicals and stay on the sidelines, so Sutton picked up a couple by throwing his jacket in the air, which ignited the Arkansas faithful.

"The joint was loaded with Razorbacks, as usual," Carter says.

Meanwhile, Sutton kept asking Prewitt, seated by the Arkansas bench, if league officials actually watched and evaluated the job SWC referees did. Prewitt finally moved seats, but the damage was done.

"The referees just wilted," Carter says, "and Arkansas blew Houston right out of the game. It was a perfect example of a coach taking complete control of the game. Here you had a bad conference that couldn't handle good basketball."

That Arkansas team featured Alvin Robertson and Scott Hastings while the UH team featured Clyde Drexler and Hakeem (then Akeem) Olajuwon. The coach's box, Carter says, was made a permanent part of the floor because of that incident.

That year, 1982, must have been a heck of a season for SWC basketball, or at least for memorable stories. WTAW's Tom Turbiville, a former A&M sports information director, was the SWC assistant information director in charge of handling the media—a task made tougher by Sutton.

All SWC practices then were closed to the media—and thus the general public—but Sutton had told a bunch of Arkansas fans that they were welcome to watch.

"I announced at the doors of Reunion Arena that practices were closed, and I was resoundingly booed by 1,000 Arkansas fans," Turbiville recalls.

Sutton wondered what all of the fuss was about and came up behind Turbiville. He told the crowd that they could come on in, and before Turbiville could draw a peep of protest, security had opened a door and the fans rushed in to see their beloved Hogs.

Funny thing was, Sutton still didn't want the media to watch. From then on practices were open to the public.

That same year just outside those same Reunion Arena doors—Turbiville says now he can tell this story—he says he had to convince Olajuwon it was illegal to scalp his complimentary game tickets.

The 6-foot, 10-inch Olajuwon, fresh from Africa and speaking little English, "couldn't understand why he couldn't scalp his comp tickets for twice their value," Turbiville says.

"Of course, getting Olajuwon mad at me was scarier than upsetting 1,000 Arkansas fans," Turbiville adds with a laugh.

Sutton probably was involved in the most intense coaching rivalry the league has ever seen. To say he and former Texas coach Abe Lemons didn't see eye to eye would be like calling Pat Buchanan mildly conservative.

"When Abe and Eddie got together, you just never knew what was going to happen," *Austin American-Statesman* columnist Kirk Bohls says.

Lemons once challenged Sutton to a fight—saying, "I was going to rip his Sunday suit"—after Sutton had gotten on to one of Lemons's players, Johnny Moore, for what he considered a cheap play.

"Those were great battles," Howard says. "Anytime they got together, you knew there were going to be sparks. And they fed off of it. It revived basketball in the Southwest Conference."

Now, SWC basketball is closing its doors to business and pleasure forever. And amid all of the hype about Texas Tech and its No. 7 ranking, the veteran reporters remind you there once was something stronger, with a following that makes the Red Raiders fans seem only semi-rabid.

MIA

In 1985 Texas A&M was playing New Mexico in "The Pit" in Albuquerque, New Mexico, in the opening round of the NIT tournament. Chip Howard met the team at the hotel the day before the game and hadn't noticed that Kenny Brown was missing. Brown was the team's leading scorer and, according to Shelby Metcalf, the finest shooter he'd ever coached.

But it seems Brown had quit the team the day before they left for what would be their final game of the season. Apparently the ultrasensitive Brown had had enough of some of the players' constant teasing and mouthing.

During those days Howard was doing a regular sportscast on early morning radio. But he had taped his sports reports for the next morning late the previous night and was going to sleep in. Imagine his surprise when A&M sports information director Tom Turbiville (now a colleague of Howard's at KZNE) knocked on the door of Howard's motel room at 5 a.m. to tell him Brown was no longer with the team.

Turbiville figured Howard needed the story for his listeners because it was appearing in the local paper that morning. So Howard did the sports news live that morning, including the strange story of Downtown Kenny Brown. Properly inspired by Brown's sudden defection, the Aggies went out that night and lost to the Lobos 80-67.

A Kid Among Legends

As a senior at Texas A&M in the fall of 1983, John Lopez, now a sports columnist for the *Houston Chronicle*, took part in the first of what would be his eight Southwest Conference press tours. He couldn't imagine a better—or more eye-opening—experience for a kid hoping to become a famous sportswriter than taking part in the legendary annual tour of SWC fall football practices.

By day, Lopez tried to apply everything he learned in class, hustling after stories, furiously scribbling every word spoken at the formally staged press conferences, and asking lots of questions of the legendary sportswriting names with whom he shared a chartered bus and wheezing prop-job airplane for 10 days.

By night, Lopez got an even better education from the likes of Blackie Sherrod, Denne Freeman, Dan Cook, and Jack Gallagher. He made it a point to spend time in hospitality rooms and dining halls as much as possible with the older generation of writers. Lopez wanted to see how they worked, what made them so well read, and gave them such staying power on the front pages of the state's biggest papers.

He learned that the best stories are the ones you can't put in the paper. He learned that scotch is good. He learned the best sources are those you get to know in social settings, not formal press conferences.

Lopez learned the best writers don't always write down every word— they listen, get a feel for what really is being said, and follow-up later with the source over a couple of beers. He learned that College Station was where *the* annual poker game was played.

Lopez watched in 1983 and 1984 and got sucked into it in 1985. And to this day, because he didn't back down from a jackass sportswriter in 1985, held his own at the table, and shared a few glasses of scotch with San Antonio columnist Dan Cook, he's still reaping the benefits.

A bit of background: Lopez originally is from San Antonio. He grew up watching Cook on the local news and reading his column in the *Express-News*. On the first two tours Lopez took around the SWC, he followed Cook around like a groupie. Cook was cool with it and always helpful, always telling stories and never acting like Lopez was a bother, which he probably was.

Lopez isn't sure if Cook actually read anything he wrote for *The Bryan-College Station Eagle*, but he said he did and said he liked it. It always made Lopez's day.

On the SWC press tour in the late summer of 1985, word was the Aggies were supposed to be pretty good. Jackie Sherrill was walking around like he had a big secret. Because Lopez was the beat writer and was at most practices, a lot of writers talked to him before doing their stories once the tour got to College Station.

Lopez hustled through his work and showed up at the annual poker game, figuring he needed to be there because it was his town. Sherrill stopped by briefly, but then left. Three of his assistant coaches stayed to play, along with several sportswriters and some sports information guys. Two tables were going at first, and Lopez wasn't playing, but then sat in when one guy left.

At Lopez's table were two A&M assistant coaches and three other writers, including a drunk sportswriter from Arkansas who seemed intent on picking a fight with everyone around him. He was an obnoxious drunk, insulting everyone, making fun of the Aggie team in front of the coaches, telling racist jokes about blacks, Hispanics, and Asians.

Around 1 a.m., there was only one table still playing poker and, remarkably, Lopez was still in with a fair stack of chips. The ass from Arkansas started challenging Lopez to one-on-one blackjack, which Lopez knew was a sucker bet. Lopez kept changing the subject and chatting with the coaches and other writers.

Everyone at the table was telling the drunk writer to shut up, but he never did. He started calling the Texans derogatory names and a couple of the guys wanted to deck him. One of the Aggie strength coaches showed up—a big, muscular guy—and told the guy from Arkansas he probably should leave. Instead, he insulted the coach.

That's when one of the Aggie assistant coaches stood up and announced, "Nobody leave. I'll be right back."

About 20 minutes later, the A&M coach returned with a roll of $20 bills the likes of which Lopez had never seen. With some urging he couldn't refuse from the weight coach and a couple other burly types who showed up, the ass from Arkansas reluctantly sat down to play the A&M coach one-on-one blackjack.

"You want to play blackjack?" the coach told him. "Then you're going to play."

About an hour later, the ass from Arkansas was cleaned out, roughed up, and too drunk to get to his room.

Lopez isn't sure how much of a factor his sticking it out with those guys helped his career, or what sharing a few drinks and listening to Cook's stories did, but less than three months later, at 23 years old, Lopez was hired at the *San Antonio Express-News*. Lopez later found out that Cook had put in a good word for him.

The day after the poker game when Lopez saw Sherrill, he winked and said, "Did you play poker last night?" For the rest of his career at A&M, Lopez had a great rapport with Jackie. Sherrill would tip Lopez off on stories and gave him plenty of insight to the league and what was going on with his team.

On the following January 1, the Aggies had won their first SWC title in nearly 20 years and beat Bo Jackson's Auburn Tigers in the Cotton Bowl. When A&M later got implicated in NCAA violations, Lopez called Sherrill's house, and although Sherrill wouldn't comment to other reporters, he gave Lopez several exclusive quotes about his thoughts on the NCAA investigation.

The coaches and strength coaches in that room went on to become some of Lopez's best sources on football. They still are today. The writers with whom Lopez shared those early press tour trips continue to be among his best friends. Lopez doesn't know what happened to the guy from Arkansas, but he figures he probably won't forget the 1985 press tour, either.

A Rhetorical Question

"Tom, have you been drinking?"

Still, two decades later, Jackie Sherrill's question rings in Tom Turbiville's ears.

It was Thanksgiving Day 1986 at Memorial Stadium in Austin, and the Aggies had just defeated the Longhorns 16-3 to win their second consecutive Southwest Conference football championship and earn their second consecutive trip to the Cotton Bowl.

Turbiville, now the sports director at KZNE radio, was in his third year as A&M's sports information director, and SIDs don't have time for postgame celebrations. That is when they earn their stripes, getting the coach on TV, getting the players to interviews, and putting out small fires here and massive blazes there.

But this postgame was different. The 1986 season had been one of controversy from the start. Quarterback Kevin Murray was the focus of a media investigation alleging his automobile (which was no Rambler) had been acquired outside of NCAA rules, and Sherrill was intent on limiting, or at the very least monitoring, his contact with the press.

At one point offensive coordinator Lynn Amadee was dispatched to sit next to Murray and a TV reporter and approve the questions before they were asked.

Fast-forward to the victory over Texas and the cramped visitors' locker room, which was packed with players, coaches, and assorted backslappers. Cotton Bowl CEO Jim Brock and his posse were making their way to the front to officially invite the Aggies to play Ohio State at Fair Park on New Year's Day.

"Hoss, where in the hell is the press?" Brock yelled Turbiville's way.

In the excitement of the moment, Sherrill had not given Turbiville the go-ahead to allow the media in. There were no reporters and no cameras to document the invitation, which was seconds away. Turbiville was holding the impatient reporters at bay outside the locker room, but Sherrill was lost amid the throng outside.

What would bring about the lesser chew from Sherrill, Turbiville asked himself: letting the media in without Sherrill's okay or not letting them in and having no video or photos of Sherrill accepting the Cotton Bowl invite? Sherrill, after all, always did enjoy a photo of Sherrill.

Alas, Turbiville chose wrong. He opened the gates to the press. They took their pictures and worse yet, surrounded Murray, who wasn't chap-

Longtime sports reporters across the state all seem to have a favorite—or not-so-favorite—Jackie Sherrill story.

eroned. Perhaps Sherrill had been angrier before and has been since, but Turbiville doubts it. Those memorable words slipped through the coach's gritted teeth.

"Tom, have you been drinking?"

Turbiville wishes he had been.

> "NO, I DIDN'T DRINK IT BEFORE THE GAME."
>
> —*Tony Barone after Texas coach Tom Penders gave him a bottle of wine before their last meeting as the basketball coaches of A&M and Texas*

The Kitty Box

Darryl Bruffett, now the sports director for KBTX-TV, once had to buy an LSU T-shirt at LSU Stadium following the Aggies' 27-0 loss to the Tigers in 1988. All he'd heard when he was trying to leave the stadium was, "Tiger Bait!" Bruffett was a young reporter and said he didn't have enough sense to not wear an A&M shirt to an out-of-town game.

At that point he figured for sure he'd get turned into gator bait if he didn't make more of an attempt to blend in with the purple and yellow. Since then he's never worn anything with A&M written on it when he's covered the Aggies on the road.

That memory is second, however, to the 1991 NCAA regional baseball tournament at Alex Box Stadium in Baton Rouge. It seemed like it was never going to stop raining, and the tournament was going to last forever. The Aggies got off to a solid start in the tournament with a pair of victories over Southwestern Louisiana and South Alabama—and then the rains came.

After a couple of games were delayed by rain during the regional's third day, the grounds crew was on standby, again, and knew that the next big downpour probably would cancel the rest of the schedule for that day. In fact, they played most of the third day with the tarp that covered the infield bunched up on the warning track in right field, so they could drag it out faster. Great theory—but it didn't work!

When the rain started to fall, it took them so long to drag the tarp from the warning track to the infield that it filled up with water in shallow right field—no pun intended—and that's where it stayed, while the infield turned into a swamp.

If that wasn't embarrassing enough, in a desperate measure, the grounds crew must have bought all of the kitty litter and absorbent within a 50-mile radius of the stadium, to try to dry things up enough to make the field playable.

Rumor was that alley cats from all over Baton Rouge converged on Alex Box that night to take care of business, and Bruffett never doubted it. All of that sour grass and kitty litter jumbled together smelled pretty awful.

The next morning A&M coach Mark Johnson's face told the story: Bruffett knew Johnson wasn't happy that the tournament officials were going to continue play instead of instead of moving the regional down the road 60 miles or so to Lafayette, Louisiana.

Not only was the infield in brutal shape because it was 90-percent kitty litter and bumpy as a washed-out riverbed, but tournament brass implemented a rule that if the ball disappeared into the outfield mud, the runner had to stop at the nearest base when the outfielder threw up his arms.

The Aggies didn't play real well at "Cat Box" Stadium after the rains came down. They lost their next two games against LSU and Southwestern Louisiana and returned to College Station with a 44-23 final record.

After that water-boggling experience, the returning players definitely developed a greater appreciation for athletics field manager Leo Goertz and the excellent job he and his crew do at Olsen Field.

The Most Complete A&M Game Ever

When reporters work at small newspapers, they take red-eye flights on no-name airlines; they stay at motels where they park in front of their room; and they rent cars that redefine the word *compact*. Not that there's anything wrong with that. In fact, Aggie alumnus Charean Williams's best stories are from those good ol' days.

In 1990, the Aggies qualified for the Holiday Bowl. That earned Robert Cessna, Larry Bowen, Tim Stanfield, and Williams, now an NFL beat writer for the *Fort Worth Star-Telegram*, a trip to San Diego to cover the game for *The Bryan-College Station Eagle*. It was such an exciting destination that Williams's mother, Cessna's wife, and Stanfield's wife also came with them.

The flight got the group there before San Diego was awake, but having never been there, they didn't waste any time. They started with whale watching. Unfortunately, the only whales they saw were the snapshots Williams's mother took of the tops of their heads. Williams spent the boat ride hanging over the side, throwing up. They did more sightseeing—come to think of it, Williams can't remember when they worked—and that night the gang went out for dinner.

Afterward, Williams is convinced they broke the world record for most passengers in a Yugo. Somehow they fit five people in that tiny car. Stanfield and his wife were contorted in the backseat.

The game, a few days later, was as memorable. It was the most complete game Williams had ever seen an A&M team play. The Aggies beat the 13th-ranked Cougars 65-14, as quarterback Bucky Richardson became the second player in Holiday Bowl history to run, catch, and pass for scores, joining BYU's Steve Young.

Richardson contributed 344 of the Aggies' bowl-record 680 total yards, with 203 passing yards, 119 rushing yards, and 22 receiving yards. Not to be outdone, the Wrecking Crew knocked Heisman Trophy winner Ty Detmer out of the game and limited the Cougars to 185 total yards, including −12 rushing.

There are other distinct memories of covering the Aggie football team for Williams. Including being stuck in an elevator at the Cotton Bowl for an hour in 1992 and missing the end of the Aggies' 10-2 loss to Florida State, being caught in an ice storm in Fort Worth in 1991 when Quentin Coryatt nearly decapitated TCU receiver Kyle McPherson, and visiting New York City for the first time in 1988 when the Aggies played Nebraska in the Kickoff Classic.

But nothing tops that San Diego trip.

An Emotional Road to Omaha

In 18 years on the Texas A&M baseball beat, Larry Bowen, a sportswriter for *The Bryan-College Station Eagle*, witnessed more goose-bump moments than any writer deserves. Among the most memorable were John Byington's great day against Texas in 1989 and the ninth-inning home runs by Steve Scarborough and Steven Truitt to win the 1999 Super Regional against Clemson.

The 1993 regional final against North Carolina was special, too. To put the drama of the day in perspective, the Aggies had reached the regional finals in 1987, 1988, 1989, and 1992, coming up just short of the College World Series. No program in the country had been as good, as long, without reaching the promised land of Omaha, Nebraska.

The Aggies broke down the door in 1993. Led by future major league pitchers Jeff Granger, Trey Moore, and Kelly Wunsch, the Aggies won the Southwest Conference championship and were picked to host the NCAA Central I Regional at Olsen Field.

A&M's regional opener against Yale was delayed by weather and lasted until 2 a.m. The place was packed anyway, and the Yale players were awestruck when the fans swayed to "The Aggie War Hymn" well after midnight.

The Aggies rolled over Yale, Lamar, and UCLA to reach the regional final with two chances to beat North Carolina and punch their ticket to Omaha. It took just one game, with the Aggies cruising to a 14-2 victory that chased away the demons of past disappointments.

Bowen has never gotten more chills from a blowout game than he did at that one. With the Aggies well ahead, A&M coach Mark Johnson took ace pitcher Jeff Granger out of the game so the fans could honor Granger in his last home game.

The Olsen Field crowd, already intoxicated on the sweet taste of regional success, gave Granger an ovation that caused more lumps in throats than a month's worth of Hallmark commercials. Granger admitted that he fought back tears as he headed to the dugout.

Olsen Field overflowed with emotions that day, and writers weren't immune. Bowen got through the postgame interviews just fine, but then he got a hug from Coach Johnson's wife, Linda. Bowen faced the same fight Granger had fought on the way to the dugout, and he lost.

Good Samaritan

During his 24-year career as a sports reporter, Olin Buchanan, the current A&M beat writer for the *Austin American-Statesman*, has met, known, and observed countless athletes on hundreds of teams at every level of competition. And not one ever impressed him as much as Rodney

Ace Jeff Granger helped propel the Aggies to the 1993 College World Series under coach Mark Johnson.

Thomas, a junior running back at Texas A&M when Buchanan took a job covering the Aggies for *The Bryan-College Station Eagle* in 1993.

Thomas's time in the 40-yard dash, rushing yardage, and accolades didn't mean that much to Buchanan—he'd known players who were faster, more productive, and received more awards—but the way in which Thomas carried himself set him far apart from most contemporary athletes.

Thomas was always polite, always cooperative, and never complained about sharing the spotlight and the football with teammates Greg Hill and Leeland McElroy. Perhaps he didn't mind sharing the spotlight because he really never needed to be in it.

Thomas was a very good running back at A&M. Had his talent and ability equaled his character and integrity, he would have been the best ever.

A&M sports information director Alan Cannon had told Buchanan when Thomas came to A&M as a high-profile running back prospect out of Groveton, Texas, that he asked for a private meeting. Cannon first thought he would be asked about plans to promote Thomas for the Heisman Trophy.

Instead, Thomas asked for tips and guidance of how to juggle the responsibilities of athletics and academics. Although quiet by nature, Thomas would tell anyone who asked about his deep Christian faith, but he conveyed it more by actions than words.

When a vending machine in the A&M athletic dormitory malfunctioned, some people took the opportunity to grab free chips and candy bars. Thomas, who was nearby, was urged to join in.

"Just a minute," he said.

After the machine had been virtually cleared out, a repairman arrived to find Thomas there, inserting coins into the slot. He was always prepared to pay the price for his team.

In Thomas's senior season of 1994, Hill, who would eventually be a first-round NFL draft choice, was suspended for the first four games, and in his absence Thomas averaged about 100 yards per game. When Hill returned, Thomas's productivity decreased and he failed to reach 1,000 yards, the running back's definition of a great season.

In fact, he never reached 1,000. He never cared, either.

The Big Chill

12th Man Magazine associate editor Rusty Burson's favorite memory of covering Texas A&M will always be the 1992 Texas Tech game at Kyle Field, when the Aggies rallied for a last-second 19-17 win and as a result, he met his wife, Vannessa, later that night because they both decided to stay in College Station to celebrate.

Working for *12th Man*, which is so closely tied to A&M, allows Burson to be totally biased in his support of A&M, which has created some warmhearted memories after the Aggie win.

After losses, however, the memories can take on a much colder classification. The coldest in Burson's memory is from the 2000 Independence Bowl. Snowflakes that were practically the size of soccer balls fell from the skies on New Year's Eve in Shreveport.

That made driving conditions the following day bad enough. But to make matters more miserable, the Aggies lost to Mississippi State and coach Jackie Sherrill, A&M's former coach, in overtime that evening and apparently someone didn't admire the 12th Man Foundation stickers on Burson's car.

Vandals busted out the passenger seat window. They didn't take anything, but they contributed to a long, cold trip back to Texas the next day. Burson placed plastic in the window to attempt to shield his wife from the icy winds. But even today, if anyone mentions the 2000 Independence Bowl to Burson's wife, they should expect an icy glare in return.

The Sway

In the Kyle Field press box, *12th Man Magazine* editor Homer Jacobs's seat is typically next to the group of visiting writers. It's always amusing to see their reaction when the press box begins to sway when "The Aggie War Hymn" is played. Apparently, they don't read the warning posted on the desk when you check into the press box area.

One writer, a female from Beaumont, was particularly overwhelmed when the box began to move. Jacobs seriously thought she was going to get sick all over his notes.

The reaction by a visiting writer to another Kyle Field event was more poignant. As the student-side decks began to fill in with red, white, and blue T-shirts for the Oklahoma State game in 2001 just after the

September 11, 2001, terrorist attacks, one sportswriter from Oklahoma murmured reverently next to Jacobs, "Wow, they're going to pull this off."

Indeed, the Aggie fans filled the stadium with a show of patriotism that still brings goose bumps to this day.

SECTION III

In the Crowd

CHAPTER ELEVEN

An Appreciation of History

Texas A&M, dedicated in 1876, is steeped in history, and in a decade of covering the Aggies I've encountered quite of a few tales from some of the old-timers who value the university's times past. Here are a few of those tales.

Aggie Fan Margaret Rudder

Margaret Rudder watched lots of Texas A&M football from the 1950s on after her husband, Earl Rudder, became A&M president. She didn't miss a home game over nearly five decades, and following the Aggies' upset of No. 2 Nebraska in October 1998, she put that one at the top of her list.

"It was kind of like the impossible dream, but it just shows what playing on your home turf means," she said. "It topped all of them as far as being incredible. I thought that after the game the way the football team went in front of the students and lifted their helmets and thanked them for their support—I thought that was a class act."

Margaret, who passed away in March 2004, was married to the measuring stick for all Aggies, Earl Rudder, for 32 years. Earl was an Aggie football letterman, a World War II hero, and A&M president.

The elegant Margaret Rudder was one of Texas A&M's all-time biggest fans.

Margaret, considered by many as one of A&M's all-time top fans, taught school in Brady, Texas, following her graduation from the University of Texas, and she and Earl were married in June 1937 at her parents' ranch.

At the wedding Earl hid his car so his buddies couldn't polish it, and he borrowed the Brady undertaker's black sedan for his and Margaret's ride from the ranch. His friends marked the paint with "Just Married," and the good wishes never completely washed off the undertaker's car.

Earl, who passed away in 1970, is generally credited with the vision of allowing women to enroll at the staid military school starting in 1963.

"Having been a [high school] football coach," Margaret later said, "Earl knew the football coach was probably having trouble recruiting because so many of the football players wanted to come where the girls are."

"YOU JUST TOLD THEM YOU WERE LOOKING FOR BASKETBALL PLAYERS, NOT LOVERS."

—Legendary Aggie basketball coach Shelby Metcalf on recruiting in the late 1950s and early 1960s to then all-male Texas A&M

A Change in the Record Books

What was the meaning of one little football game? Perhaps plenty, if it was the first one ever played by the Texas A&M team, and all of the history books had it wrong until 1997.

Before that year, just about every record of Aggie football listed A&M's first game in history as a 14-6 victory over Galveston Ball High School in 1894. That simply wasn't the case, as pointed out by astute Aggie Newton Lamb, Class of 1960.

Through his research in the mid-1990s, Lamb found in the *Galveston Daily News* that the Aggies had actually played a football game at the University of Texas in 1894, before they'd played Ball High. And dreadfully A&M lost in a manner in which the school later prided itself on not ever happening: by quitting.

"The game of football this evening between the university and agricultural and mechanical college elevens resulted in a victory by the former by a score of 38 to 0, the second half of the game having been called off before it was played by request of the agricultural and mechanical boys," the *Galveston Daily News* reported. "The latter played well, but the

Varsity team was too heavy for them and outclassed them in every respect."

The Aggies even fumbled on their first play. But perhaps because of their misfortunes in that first game, many of the A&M faithful will claim, the Aggies never quit again, even if they were outscored plenty as they established a program that has grown into one of the nation's most prominent.

A&M stayed the valiant underdog against the more established Longhorn program until 1902. That was when the Aggies defeated UT in Austin 11-0 under former coach J.E. Platt.

The teams didn't play in College Station until 1915, when the Aggies rolled to a 13-0 victory. Legend has it the next year UT came up with the Bevo nickname for its Longhorn mascot—because it had to. Apparently A&M students had branded it with the "13-0" final, and Texas students responded by turning the score into "Bevo."

NOVEMBER 26, 1998
HOW ORANGEBLOODS AND AGGIES EVOLVE

Texas A&M quarterback Randy McCown owns the kind of picture that Texas coach Mack Brown mentions.

"We have some of our recruits' parents bring pictures of the kid when he was 2, and he's wearing a Longhorn shirt," Brown said. "I tell them, 'I wish you would have told me that sooner, I wouldn't have sent him so many notes if I would have known he was coming here anyway.'"

So goes Aggie coach R.C. Slocum's and Brown's "Predisposed" theory. A tiny Texan is born and he wears maroon or orange diapers.

"I think there are some recruits who probably got swayed by the attention on the school that year, but by and large, from what we've seen guys usually like one or the other more," Brown said. "I think the guys are kind of separated at birth. It depends on who in the family pulls them to the orange or pulls them to the maroon."

Not so fast with McCown, who's from Jacksonville, Texas.

"I wanted to be a basketball player and play at Texas," McCown said. "I even have a picture from

Christmas with me holding up a jacket with 'Texas' on it. And then in high school I actually visited the town of Austin, and I said there was no way in the world I was going to play basketball, football, or checkers there.

"I mean, Sixth Street is a cool place to visit, but there was no way I was going to live there."

So goes Slocum's "What You're Looking For" theory.

"Some will say Austin's just too crowded and they felt more comfortable at A&M," Slocum said. "Or, there's nothing to do [in College Station], and there's a great nightlife [in Austin]. It depends on what you're looking for. There are guys that you couldn't drag to Austin, and there are guys you couldn't drag to College Station. I just want to keep the good ones here in Texas."

So goes Slocum's and Brown's "Keep the Good Ones in Texas" proverb.

"It's more important that they want to stay in-state after this game is played, and want to play in this game, than which one of the two schools they choose," Brown said.

When Slocum recruited former Texas quarterback Shea Morenz of San Angelo, he said that Morenz liked everything about A&M—except that it had "A&M" attached to "Texas."

"But I knew that going in," Slocum said.

So it went for UT linebacker Dusty Renfro of Alvarado, Texas.

"I pretty much had my eyes set on Texas since I can remember," Renfro said. "My dad was always a big Longhorn fan. He was a senior in high school in 1969 when they won the national championship."

But there also are a few rebels in this year's bunch.

"My uncle [James Denton] was head of the poultry science department at A&M," said UT offensive lineman Jay Humphrey of Richardson. "And so every birthday and Christmas I knew what I was going to get—A&M paraphernalia." But he visited Austin and "fell in love with the place."

Aggie punter Shane Lechler had his heart set on Texas because his second cousin, Ty Harrington, played baseball for the Longhorns.

"When I was in elementary school and junior high I was going to Texas, no doubt," Lechler said.

Then in 1993 he attended Aggie Bonfire and the A&M–Texas game at Kyle Field, when Aggie safety Dennis Allen intercepted Morenz in the end zone late in the fourth quarter.

The Aggie atmosphere convinced Lechler, who was recruited as a quarterback/punter, that A&M was the place to be. It didn't help UT when a Texas assistant called with a recruiting pitch.

"He said, 'Shane, we've got some good quarterbacks here. Would you mind playing fullback?'" Lechler said. "So I just went into my room where I had a list of teams and scratched them right off."

Texas defensive back Joe Walker said that he liked A&M's colors growing up in Galena Park, Texas.

"Colors were a big thing," he said. "And I really liked A&M's and Florida State's colors." But he picked the burnt orange after visiting Austin. See the "W.Y.L.F." theory.

Aggie offensive lineman Cameron Spikes loved Texas as a big kid in Bryan.

"I bled burnt orange," he said. "My father was a big Texas fan and Texas football was all I knew growing up. I never paid much attention to A&M, maybe because it was right here. But I'm glad I came to A&M."

None of the guys—imagine this—said they wished they had played for the other school. So goes the "Post-Predisposed" theory.

Crowd Control

In 1978 the Texas women's basketball team showed up at G. Rollie White Coliseum to play and noticed a line of cadets outside the arena. The team couldn't believe that they were going to have a crowd that large watch them play.

"This is going to be wild," head coach Jody Conradt thought as she looked at the line. "We have never played in front of more than 200 people."

But then the game started, and the stands were full of stragglers. Coach Conradt thought it was an Aggie joke, and so she forgot about the crowd and focused on the game.

Her team took a large lead when suddenly they opened the doors and floods of people came pouring into the arena. It was packed beyond anything the Longhorn team had ever seen.

"We completely freaked out and lost the game," Conradt recalled, "and that was the last game we lost for 12 years in the Southwest Conference."

Hard Knocks

Once back when radio personality Chip Howard was calling basketball games, A&M was playing Pan-American, and one of the opposing players threw an elbow and knocked Mike Clifford's tooth right out in front of him on the broadcast bench.

Those two players had been trailing the play, and the officials didn't know it had happened until Clifford went and picked up the tooth and showed it them.

A New Era for Aggie Football

Few realized it then, but a groundbreaking era dawned the morning after New Year's Day 1972. That's when Emory Bellard, only days on the job as Texas A&M's football coach, delivered a straightforward message to his new staff.

"I gave everyone a list of names to recruit, and our philosophy was to look for good young men and good football players," Bellard recalled. "We weren't going to settle for anything less than that."

Based on those beliefs, Bellard's first recruiting class included eight African Americans. It marked the first time an A&M coach heavily pursued blacks.

"We didn't intentionally go after black athletes. We went after the best athletes we could find," Bellard said. "It turned out that some were black and some were white."

Bellard's fresh approach to recruiting football players to Texas A&M paid off handsomely. In 1974, A&M won eight games for the first time since 1957—coach Paul "Bear" Bryant's last season in College Station—

based on Bellard's mantra of pursuing the best athletes possible, regardless of color.

Decades later, A&M players still say they appreciative Bellard's initiative.

"He did a great thing by recruiting African Americans," Aggie safety Japhus Brown said. "I might not be here today if he hadn't. That couldn't have been easy on those guys. They had a lot of guts to come here."

When the Aggies wrapped up their football season 30 years ago, they didn't receive the kind of praise that comes with having a breakout campaign—and for good reason. Texas had owned the Southwest Conference for six of the previous seven seasons.

The SWC's surprise team in 1974 was Baylor, which won the conference title. But A&M also made it a season to remember, beating LSU and Washington on the road and defeating Arkansas at home.

That season, Hugh McElroy sat in the Kyle Field stands and smiled at a new collection of players making their mark at A&M. In 1970, McElroy was the first black to start and score a touchdown for the Aggies, under then-coach Gene Stallings.

"I took pride in showing that it could be done," said McElroy, who lettered at A&M from 1970 to 1971. "I had no grand scheme or plan or anything like that. I was just glad to accomplish something that others could point to and say, 'Here's a kid who's at a school that, in the past, hadn't done much outreach.'"

Stallings, whose seven-year Aggie ledger included a rare A&M conference title in 1967, said he tried to recruit black athletes to A&M in the 1960s but had little luck. Stallings won a 1992 national championship at Alabama with a team composed largely of African Americans.

A&M wasn't the only school behind the curve when it came to recruiting black players. The SWC didn't have an African-American football player on scholarship until the mid-1960s, when Jerry LeVias rose to stardom at SMU.

"There were a lot of injustices that took place everywhere years ago—just things that had existed for a long time," Bellard said. "We didn't pay any attention to any of those."

In 1974—driven by such star talents as Thomas, safety Lester Hayes, and running back Bubba Bean—the Aggies were 8-2 headed into their final game at Texas. But the Longhorns won 32-3 behind freshman Earl Campbell's 127 rushing yards.

In 1975, Bellard's first recruiting class, seniors by now, led A&M to a share of the conference crown, thanks largely to a swift defense that placed all 11 starters in the NFL.

"Every one of those guys could run," Bellard said, "and every one was as tough as a wood hauler."

Carl Torbush, the Aggies' defensive coordinator, witnessed A&M's mid-1970s might firsthand. He was a graduate assistant at Baylor at the time.

"That was as fine a defense as I've ever seen," Torbush said, "and I've coached a lot of football."

Building upon their success of 1974, the Aggies rose to a No. 2 ranking in 1975 and beat UT for the first time since 1967. But a stunning 31-6 loss at Arkansas in A&M's final regular-season game squashed the Aggies' hopes of securing the school's second national title.

Asked the reason for the Aggies' rapid turnaround in the early 1970s, former Longhorn coach Darrell Royal offered a succinct answer.

"Emory," Royal said of his former assistant. "He was just a fine coach and fine recruiter, one of the best I've ever been around."

Bellard, retired and living in Georgetown, compiled a 48-27 record over six seasons at A&M. He might have made his biggest mark, however, by shoving open doors that previously had only been cracked in College Station.

And for that, even today's players say they're grateful—to Bellard and to the first African-American recruits to don the maroon and white of A&M.

"You've got to respect the people who paved the way for you," Aggie linebacker Justin Warren said. "If those guys hadn't have come here first, I might be going through what they did. Or I wouldn't have been here, period."

Championship Rings—Five Decades Later

Does anyone doubt that God has a sense of humor? Call it the lighter side of divine intervention.

How else do you explain the Aggies beating their highest-ranked opponent to that point in history for Texas A&M football in the presence of a bunch of old God-fearing men whose record they broke? The 1939 national champions—forever glorified for gridiron and world war prowess—defeated No. 4 Tulane in the 1940 Sugar Bowl.

And on a glorious October day in Aggieland in 1998, A&M defeated No. 2 Nebraska 28-21 at Kyle Field. The youngsters, too, treated the old-timers to an amazing game in what was the first official "Maroon Out" at Kyle—where all of the home fans wore the school's primary color. One writer said Kyle looked like a stirred fire ant bed that day.

"It was a sea of maroon," a triumphant Aggie senior safety Rich Coady said.

Earlier in the day, the school honored the 1939 team by presenting the remaining members or their survivors with national championship rings. Fifty-nine isn't a likely reunion year, but there was good reason A&M honored the 1939 Aggies in 1998 instead of 1999.

"We lost two to death last year and two the year before," team member Howard Shelton said. "We needed to get on with it."

Nineteen of the surviving players were honored at a ceremony in old G. Rollie White Coliseum before that day's game against Nebraska. G. Rollie had closed the year before to basketball after serving for 44 years as the sport's home, but the coliseum was still 15 years from opening when the 1939 gridiron heroes finished 11-0 with a 14-13 victory over Tulane in the Sugar Bowl.

The 1939 gang is a mythical bunch, still hailed by a "National Champions 1939" declaration in raised letters across the upper deck of Kyle Field. In a different era for football, just about every player was pegged with a nickname—and the Aggies' 1939 roster was dotted with the likes of Pinky, Uncle Bill, Bama, Jitterbug, Dog, Cotton, and Buck.

But no one was more renowned than broad-shouldered running back Jarrin' John Kimbrough of the West Texas town of Haskell. That day in 1998, the steel-blue eyes of Kimbrough glowed among his old teammates.

"This is just wonderful," Kimbrough said, smiling. "I still call them boys, but they're really all old men, just like me."

Sportswriter Jinx Tucker honored the 1939 squad when it won the national title, and his words are timeless:

"When the days of 1939 are but a vivid memory, you can take your grandchildren on your respective knees, take out the tattered scrapbook, the newspaper clippings yellowed with age, and tell how you were an integral part of a machine that was recognized not only throughout the state of Texas, but from the Atlantic Coast to the Pacific Slope as the most devastating, most powerful and most destructive football machine that waded through a representative schedule in that year.

"Your deeds will live and live until they become a legend as sacred to the traditions of the old school as is the historic Kyle Field that you played on."

The shiny new rings, too, seemed the perfect fit of a lifetime for worn, pleased hands.

The Two Bums

Split by a half-century of the Texas–Texas A&M rivalry, a Bum was still a Bum—a beautiful burnt maroon mix of grandfather and grandson.

The elder Bum once donned burnt orange, while his grandson chose maroon. The ascendant picked No. 81 five decades ago—the other later proudly bore it in his grandpa's honor. Each earned the nickname "Bum" from teammates—two men drawn to the same game and only distanced by generations.

Separated by 50 years of football on the same glorious fields, Max and Matt Bumgardner were two examples of how UT and A&M—split by 90 miles of pasture and supposedly a world of ideology—were more alike than different.

That was especially evident in the weeks following the tragic fall of A&M's Bonfire in November 1999, when Matt Bumgardner was a senior receiver on the Aggies. It was during A&M's most trying time after the collapse claimed the lives of 12 members of the 12th Man—that UT embraced its grieving, hurting neighbor like never before.

Like family. Like Max and Matt Bumgardner.

Max caught quarterback Bobby Layne's passes for Texas in the late 1940s. In fact, he caught more passes than any other Longhorn in 1947 and became a first-round draft pick of the Chicago Bears. Matt caught one of A&M's biggest passes in history in the 1998 Big 12 championship game, when his diving grab of a 30-yarder from Branndon Stewart kept a late drive alive against Kansas State.

A year later, Matt caught the winning touchdown pass in the Aggies' 20-16 upset of UT in what's known as the Bonfire Game at Kyle Field.

Matt was torn between A&M and Texas out of Luling High School. Well aware of his grandfather's exploits—captaining the 1947 team to a 10-1 finish and a top 5 ranking—Matt's heart still beat for A&M. He visited Texas and became even more hesitant about picking a school. Then Grandpa called.

"He said nothing would make him prouder for me to go to Texas," Matt said. "But he also said A&M is a great place, too, and I'd do just as well there."

Max had spent seven years at A&M as athletic dorm supervisor and academic adviser, so he knew the strengths of both schools.

"Now, if he would have told me, 'I want you to go to Texas,' I would have gone, just out of respect for him," Matt said. "But with him saying both places were great, it kind of left it up to me."

Before Matt played his first game at A&M, Max made his own decision: that he wouldn't leave the side of his wife, whose health was failing. Not even for a day, and not even for their grandson's games in the same stadiums in which he once played.

When visiting his grandparents as a child, Matt would beg Max to show him his old Texas and Chicago Bears gear and College All-Star game jersey. Grandpa also told him stories about World War II, about how the platoon from which he was transferred was later completely wiped out in the Battle of the Bulge.

Max started his football career at Texas in 1941 but like others of his generation soon joined the war. He served more than three years in the Army in Germany, England, and France before returning to Texas.

Max's first coach at Texas was the legendary D.X. Bible, who also had coached at A&M. As a senior in 1947, Max played for Blair Cherry and caught 15 passes for 234 yards as the Longhorns lost one game, by a single point, to SMU and its star running back, Doak Walker.

But after what Max had seen in the war, losing a football game wasn't the end of the world. And the annual A&M game wasn't the ends to all means, either, although Max quickly mentioned his teams always beat the Aggies.

"You just didn't like A&M at all," Max said, laughing. "But I love them now, I sure do."

When Matt came to A&M, he grabbed No. 81 at first chance, as a tribute to Max. Max even signed his letters to Matt, "Old No. 81."

Aggie coach R.C. Slocum was asked if he ever slipped and called Matt by his grandpa's name.

"No, I called him Bum," Slocum said, smiling. "And that's what we called his grandpa."

Matt Bumgardner recorded one of the most memorable catches in A&M history against Kansas State in the Big 12 title game.

Bonfire Remembered

One by one, Texas A&M players somberly showed up for practice at Kyle Field on that sad day of November 18, 1999. Less than 12 hours earlier, at 2:42 a.m., the Aggie Bonfire stack collapsed while under construction, killing 12 volunteers, 11 of them students. Another 27 were injured.

As the heavy-hearted players filed into their Kyle Field locker room, none had the stomach for practice, even with a showdown against archrival Texas just eight days away. Gone was any obsession with football heroics. The Aggie football team just wanted to help.

"We showed up [at the Bonfire site] and said, 'We're here to help. We know that we can,'" Randy McCown, then A&M's senior quarterback, recalled. "We all agreed that's what we needed to do."

The players, with the permission of their ashen-faced coach R.C. Slocum, had headed across campus for the Bonfire site. In one of the most commendable efforts seen from a college football team, the Aggies spent hours carrying away logs that had been gingerly removed from the collapsed stack by rescuers trying to recover the bodies of victims.

"Those boys were doing anything and everything they could to help out," recalled longtime A&M police chief Bob Wiatt, now retired.

Chris Valletta, the team's center, still owns a worn, dirty cap from that day on which he wrote, "Nov. 18, 1999—Never Forget."

"We were just exhausted, but that didn't even enter our minds, because we heard that people were still under there," Valletta said. "Everybody was covered in mud. I'll always remember that one of the Redpots [a student Bonfire worker] came up to me with a hard hat turned upside down and filled with water, and we all drank from it. The unity that day was unbelievable."

The following week an underdog A&M team rallied from a 10-point halftime deficit to defeat seventh-ranked UT 20-16 in an emotion-filled game played before 86,128. At halftime, the Longhorn band played "Amazing Grace." The Aggie band followed with a "Silent T" formation. As the A&M band slowly marched off the field, the only sound in the stadium was the crying of babies.

"We were just a bunch of kids, but a lot of the players took it upon themselves to win that game," said receiver Matt Bumgardner, who caught the winning touchdown pass from McCown in the game's closing minutes.

"It was a lot of pressure to put on ourselves, and it was a real emotional time for everybody. That game was a lot different from other A&M-Texas games. There was a lot of respect from both sides, and there wasn't any taunting. When we came out of the locker room at halftime, 86,000 people were dead silent. It was surreal."

Added McCown: "Of any game I've ever played, I just knew we were going to win that one. Even when we were behind at halftime, I never felt anxious. I just knew we were going to win. Everybody knew what needed to take place."

To mark the fifth anniversary of the tragedy, A&M dedicated a memorial in November 2004 on the site of the collapse.

CHAPTER TWELVE

The Roar of
the 12th Man

In the winter of 2005 I solicited favorite and memorable A&M athletics stories from Aggies on the popular website texags.com. I received many wonderful responses, and here are a few of those stories in chronological order.

CHARLES STAGG, CLASS OF 1970, ALVIN

The Catch

The year was 1967, and the season was tumultuous. It began with a nationally televised game against SMU at Kyle Field, which I watched on my father's new 25-inch color television. Twenty-five inches—wow! It was impressive.

Back when there was only one college game on TV each week and every now and then a doubleheader, having your team on the tube was a real treat. With only a few ticks left on the clock, the Ags jumped ahead of the Ponies, but, alas, SMU's Jerry LeVias—the first African-American scholarship player in the Southwest Conference—got the last laugh when he not only returned the ensuing kickoff to midfield, but also caught a touchdown late in the game in a 20-17 Mustangs victory.

What a letdown. Every year back then we would say, "Wait until next year!" We had been outscored frequently, but hope always sprang eternal in the "wait until next year" world of the Aggies. This was a new year—a next year, if you will—and the start wasn't great. LeVias later said that he didn't remember what happened after that kickoff return, because he got his bell rung on the play.

So in the most stunning play of the game, the most important participant wasn't even aware of what he'd done. That made the bad taste doubly bitter. We played our next three games against nonconference foes and lost them all—and we were 0-4. It looked like another disappointing year.

But with many of my classmates and friends already claiming, "Wait until next year," I hadn't given up hope. If we could win out, we would still be SWC champions and claim our rightful place in the beloved Cotton Bowl. "Keep fighting," I thought.

As we progressed through the conference schedule, the Fightin' Texas Aggies held their heads high. We won every league game leading up to the Thanksgiving showdown with Texas. It was an odd year (1967), so we were privileged to play at Kyle Field, and all of the seating was on one deck back then.

My ticket for the game was in the horseshoe on the stadium's north end—dead center, right behind the goalposts. My girlfriend was with me, and she had never attended an Aggie game. It was a big day for me—and it turned out to be a big day for the Ags. Kyle Field held about 49,000 fans then, and every seat was filled—even the ones on the track that were so low you couldn't really see the action.

We led by a field goal before Texas quickly countered with a touchdown to lead by four. I could feel the despair in the air. That sickening feeling in the pit of your stomach—if you're truly a fan—was making its presence known. Then, suddenly, it happened in the fourth quarter.

On the second play from scrimmage from our own 20-yard line, quarterback Edd Hargett passed to Bob Long. I can still see it as if it happened today. Those end zone horseshoe seats gave me the perfect angle on a perfect pass.

Hargett's beauty of a throw sailed down the middle of the field and a little toward the right sideline—right over Long's shoulder into his outstretched hands, and he outran those teasips all the way to the end zone. Final score: A&M 10, t.u. 7.

The Cotton Bowl was sweet because it matched A&M coach Gene Stallings against his former coach and mentor, Paul "Bear" Bryant of Alabama. The Aggies won 20-16 on New Year's Day 1968 as I watched from the living room of my dad's home in front of his sparkling new 25-inch TV.

But I'll never forget how we "sawed Varsity's horns off" on Thanksgiving Day 1967. Nobody wanted to leave the stands—we wanted that moment to live forever. It does in the memories of those of us who were lucky enough to be in the crowd that day.

CHASE HOLLAND, CLASS OF 1969, SAN ANGELO

A Coach's Appreciation for Senior Boots

In 1968 I was a senior, and as was the custom of the day, in the Corps of Cadets. Three or four of the seniors from Squadron 5 (Filthy Fifth) liked to go watch football practice in the afternoons. We usually were on the sidelines standing beside the players not directly involved in that particular drill.

Because coach Gene Stallings had led us to a Cotton Bowl victory over Bear Bryant's Alabama team with Ken Stabler at quarterback the previous season, we all had high expectations for that fall.

With the likes of Edd Hargett, Rolf Krueger, Tommy Maxwell, Tom Buckman, Ross Brupbacher, and Billy Hobbs returning, we certainly didn't expect to go 3-7 for the season (which was what we wound up doing). After a frustrating beginning to the year, Coach Stallings closed practices to all spectators and the media.

One particular day two other seniors and I from the Filthy Fifth showed up, as usual, in uniform. One of the student trainers, trying to do his job, was in a heated discussion with us about attending what was supposed to be a closed practice.

Coach Stallings—as if he had nothing else to do—came over to see what the problem was. He was told we were being asked to leave practice. Coach pointed to our Senior Boots, which we wore every day, and said to the trainer, "Son, you see those boots? If someone is wearing those, he's damn sure on our side. They can come any time, and they can stay as long as they'd like."

We certainly felt important, thanks to Coach Stallings's love for Texas A&M and its traditions.

GARY HILL, CLASS OF 1974, SAN ANTONIO

The MOB Out of Line

In the 1973 game at Rice, the Owls held a 17-0 lead going into halftime. We had beaten SMU 45-10 the week before to go 5-4 for the season, and serious rumors had us getting an invite to the Peach Bowl if we beat Rice.

I was a member of the Aggie Band, and as we stood in the north end zone awaiting the last couple of minutes of the first half, Rice's Marching Owl Band was gathered along the stadium's west side, down near us and close to me. The MOB had some mouthy types who were "wishing us well" as we stood in silence.

Aggie fans above them in the stadium were voicing their displeasure with the MOB's antics toward us. Being the focus of verbal abuse in that era was nothing new to us, so it was pretty much ignored. Many of the kids in the MOB were not Rice students but high school band members recruited to flesh out the show.

We had several guys in the Aggie Band from Houston who had walked in a Rice band halftime show while they were still in high school. The MOB concept of chicanery was new for that year and had gained some notice a few weeks prior for its performance at Memorial Stadium in Austin.

What we considered witty toward t.u. was turning ugly toward A&M. We did our drill and ran off—the normal stuff. As we moved back into the stadium seats the MOB started its show. Their first image was a boot, meant to be an A&M Senior Boot.

The announcer talked about how it was used to step in cow manure or something along those lines. This got the overwhelmingly A&M crowd irritated and started the hissing and booing. Next formation was a fire hydrant with the majorettes roaming around with empty dog collars on leashes, with the MOB playing, "Oh where, oh where has my little dog gone?"

Reveille had just been put down, and the intent was obvious. That got more booing. Next formation was a chicken leg. Noted Houston television personality Marvin Zindler came out and did a very good twirling routine. Zindler, he of *The Best Little Whorehouse in Texas* fame, had spearheaded a "crusade" the previous spring to shut down the Chicken Ranch (a whorehouse) in La Grange, Texas.

That got major laughs from the crowd and settled things down, mostly. The MOB then wandered to the north end zone and mimicked the FTAB block band formation, but in Nazi goosestep style, and played a poor version of "The Aggie War Hymn."

At that point the crowd erupted, and one 40-ish guy in a red shirt went onto the field and decked a saxophone-playing MOB member. The Aggie Band officers on duty were working to keep folks in the stands. A purple smoke grenade showed up on the field and one of the ODs (Squadron 7 had the duty that game) and longtime personal friend of mine picked up the grenade and hurled it into the empty seat section in the north end zone.

Our White Band drum major signaled for us to play "The Aggie War Hymn," which we did. It drowned out the MOB, and its marching formation fell apart, and they decided to trudge off the field and back to the southwest part of the stands from whence they originally came.

The stands then Sawed Varsity's Horns Off—especially loud that time. We were all pretty upset at the MOB. We sent the dorkiest fish in the FTAB down to the MOB with a message telling them that we would not guarantee its members' safety after the game.

The Aggies made a great comeback, only to lose the lead late in the game and fall 24-20 to despised Rice. It was the worst football loss in my four years. Amazingly, after the game the MOB had to be removed from its *own* stadium in police paddy wagons. A couple of days later, the same guys from Squadron 7 went down to Houston and chopped down the Rice victory tree.

I've seen my friend's brass-labeled momento of the occasion on his fireplace many times. The next year for the game at Kyle the MOB was not invited to perform at halftime, and A&M pounded out a 37-7 victory over the institute.

Emory Bellard (left) was the first A&M football coach to heavily recruit African-American players.

KYLE FOSTER, CLASS OF 1998, PORT ARTHUR

Running With the Big Boys

My family moved from Port Arthur to Bryan in 1971. That fall my father took me to my first Aggie football game, and we even ate at a legendary burger joint, Dead Solid Perfect, beforehand.

Fast-forward to 1975. I was 12 years old, and Emory Bellard was the Aggies' football coach. He had a son named Bobby, who was a few years older than me. Back then the Aggies practiced on Kyle Field on Astroturf, and practices were open to the public.

Students sat in the stands studying and watching and so forth. Well, the neighborhood kids all went up to Kyle regularly to play touch football in the area that is now where the aluminum stands are in front of the JumboTron. So we'd play football and made a career out of getting sweatbands from the players.

Getting to pat Bubba Bean, George Woodard, Bucky Sams, Richard Osborne, and the like on the arm and say, "Beat the hell outta whomever!"—well, those were the days. Can you imagine playing touch football as a 12-year-old while the A&M football team was practicing on the same field? People ask me why I love being an Aggie so much.

I just laugh and say, "How could I be anything else?"

PETE MARKEY, CLASS OF 1987, ORANGE

The Block

In 1984 classmate Chuck Morris and I headed to Austin for the annual football clash between our beloved Texas Aggies and the despised Longhorns. It was the last day of November, and A&M was coming off of a surprising victory against TCU at Kyle Field. The teasips still had a shot at the Cotton Bowl.

We met up with a few high school chums at T.C. Jester dorm and proceeded to take all kinds of abuse from the pro-Longhorn crowd the night before the game. All evening and on into the next day we defended our honor and our school. The game was a nationally televised ESPN special, so the majority of the day was spent drinking, dodging thrown eggs, yelling and receiving obscenities, and drinking some more.

After a sumptuous fish sandwich at Mickey-D's (McDonald's), we headed to Memorial Stadium. The first half was magical. A&M dominated in every facet of the game, and we led 20-0. Chuck and I were in a state of shock and euphoria, and in our exuberance we each even got in a tussle in the men's room before racing out for the second-half kickoff.

Texas came out after halftime and drove the ball down the field. With the crowd into it, A&M held, and the field goal team came out. I leaned over to Chuck and screamed, "Domingo will block that sucker!"

Hallelujah, it happened—Domingo Bryant did, indeed, block the kick. Scott Polk returned the ball 76 yards to the Texas seven-yard line, as a big part of the crowd headed for the exits. It was incredible to be in

Memorial Stadium that day and see only the fourth victory ever for A&M there.

All night long Aggies were singing "The Aggie War Hymn" up and down Sixth Street. It made me proud to be part of such a great tradition and such a great family.

MARTY TATE, CLASS OF 1988, SPRING

Something to Yell About

My all-time favorite memory of Kyle Field is the 1985 Texas game. This was back in the days when the north end of Kyle was a horseshoe of the old first deck, and the stadium had an official capacity of 72,000, although that night a then-record 77,607 fans packed into the stadium.

The game was played on Thanksgiving night, the way it should be, and a new all-sports network called ESPN was beginning to catch on. Coach Jackie Sherrill and the Aggies were one of its favorite football teams to showcase.

A&M and t.u. were playing for the Southwest Conference championship and the right to go to the Cotton Bowl—back when it really meant something. It was a clear, cool night, and there was definitely electricity in the air.

I've never heard Kyle Field louder than it was that night, when Kevin Murray, Roger Vick, and the founding fathers of the Wrecking Crew defense dominated the Longhorns 42-10. As the game drew to a close, fans began throwing cotton in the air—it was literally raining cotton at Kyle.

As if anything could top that experience, just about every Aggie in the stadium headed over to the Northgate bar district afterward. The crowd overflowed from the Dixie Chicken and Duddley's Draw into University Drive. The police wisely barricaded the area between the post office and the Chicken, and let the crowd have some fun.

Eventually, the crowd was called to attention by the sound of the Parson's Mounted Calvary firing off a few rounds from the field artillery in the parking lot just across the street from the Chicken.

Some yell leaders also somehow made it up onto the roof of the Chicken and Duddley's and began conducting one of the most memorable yell practices I've ever been privileged to be a part of. It seems like yesterday.

STEWART ROWLAND, CLASS OF 1992, IRVING

Olsen Magic

Back in 1988, I was just a clueless freshman still trying to find my way around campus and understand what Texas A&M was all about. Because of a lack of on-campus housing, I was living in an apartment with three buddies from high school. Being off-campus, I missed out on a lot of the Aggie experience.

Even though I was and am a huge sports fan, I actually missed two football games that year and went to very few basketball games.

Then, in the later winter of 1989, I attended my first Aggie baseball game. I was immediately hooked. Every aspect of Aggie baseball was top notch, from Olsen Field to the Raggies to the Diamond Darlings to D.D. Grubbs on the PA to all that skill on the diamond. With every blowout win or come-from-behind victory, my enthusiasm grew for the top-ranked Aggies. And the Aggie spirit began to capture me.

The season began to draw to an end, and the big series with the Longhorns was upon us. We were all disappointed when Mother Nature delayed the first game of the series to Saturday night and even more disappointment came when Kirk Dressendorfer put on a terrific performance to take Game 1 for the No. 10 Longhorns.

However, in the bottom of the ninth, John Byington gave us all a preview of what was to come the following day when he homered deep to left field.

We arrived to the ballpark early the next day to grab the front row on the first base side. The game was to be televised, and I had called my parents to make sure they were going to watch the game and set the VCR. Despite the loss the previous night, there was electricity in the air when the Ags batted around in the bottom of the first and scored seven runs.

Texas battled back, but Terry Taylor hit a two-run blast to the original Aggie Alley that extended the A&M lead once again. Then things started to go awry. A&M shortstop Chuck Knoblauch got booted for arguing a call, and Texas eventually took a 14-9 lead to the bottom of the ninth.

John Byington hit two of A&M's most memorable home runs in history—on the same day of a doubleheader against Texas.

That's when things went crazy. The Ags started getting base hits, and the Longhorns began playing like the Bad News Bears. Suddenly, the game was tied 14-14 with the bases loaded and Big John Byington at the plate. It felt like Olsen Field was about to crumble from all of the ruckus. The bleachers we were sitting on didn't seem like they were attached to the concrete anymore, and the noise was deafening.

Dressendorfer, after throwing about 150 pitches the night before, came out of the pen for the Longhorns. His outing in this game was a little shorter—one pitch. Byington, much like the night before, crushed his fastball deep to left field for a grand slam and an 18-14 victory. The raw emotion and energy at that moment can't be described in words.

To this day, I get chills just thinking about it. The most unbelievable thing is there was more to come. Later that same night, Byington did the same thing. Tied 5-5 in the bottom of the ninth, Byington sent Chris Gaskill's first pitch, a curveball, over the left-field wall to hand A&M an 8-5 win and keep the Aggies ranked No. 1 in the country.

It was the single greatest day of my Aggie life. Some might argue that the 1998 Big 12 championship football game, the 1999 Texas football game, or the 2002 football Oklahoma game was better. But, for me that Sunday doubleheader will remain as the single defining moment in my Aggie life.

SCOTT WOOD, CLASS OF 1994, SAN MARCOS

Olsen Magic from Beyond the Fence

My junior year in high school was the year A&M had arguably its best team ever in baseball—certainly the best team it had to that date. It was 1989, and Aggie baseball was on a tear.

And even though the Aggies were heading into their annual series with t.u. as the No. 1-ranked team in the country, there was still the challenge ahead of overcoming their inability to beat Texas in almost any sport—an inability we had only recently overcome in football.

There was still a chain-link fence along the left-field wall at Olsen at this time, and you had to get there early to get a good seat. My brother and I grabbed a spot just along the left-field line and sat through a disappointing 6-2 loss in the opener.

That loss set up the greatest sports memory of my life to date. We once again took our spot sitting just beyond the outfield wall for the second game, and frustration with another loss to the 'sips quickly turned into elation, as the Ags jumped out to a 7-0 lead. The top team in the country looked like it would bounce back with a fury and take Game 2 easily.

Unfortunately, the Aggies would squander that lead in a game that had Texas leading 14-9 going into the bottom of the ninth. Frustrated in the middle of the game, I left the "comfort" of the fence and laid down and listened to Dave South on the radio for a couple of innings—only to be awakened again, as future major league Rookie of the Year Chuck Knoblauch was thrown out of the game.

After an emotionally trying game—and as every good Aggie knows—A&M came back to win that one 18-14 on a John Byington grand slam. With the crowd on the edge of its seat (or on the edge of the fence), Texas ace Kirk Dressendorfer came in to face Byington with the bases loaded.

First pitch ... ping! I jumped up off of the fence—and ran toward the scoreboard (still in left field) knowing that the hit would prove historical. I ended up wrestling with two other Aggies for the game ball, and although I didn't walk away with it, I got up and hugged the other guy who had unsuccessfully fought for the winning ball. I then proceeded to run around the outfield fence high-fiving every person in maroon.

The crowd was going crazy. I've not heard that level of excitement at any event since—including Game 7 of the Rockets–Suns series in 1992 or A&M football games against Texas, Arkansas, or any other opponent. And to this day, that moment with me following the trajectory of Byington's shot heard round the state remains my most vivid and exciting memory of Aggie sports.

You'll still catch me at home football games visiting the Aggie Hall of Fame and watching that clip over and over again. Thanks to the team of 1989 for the goose bumps!

KEVIN WORLEY, CLASS OF 1991, AMARILLO

The Twist

In October 1992 Texas A&M played Texas Tech at Kyle Field. My wife had to work that day, and I somehow allowed her to convince me to tape the game and we would watch it together when she came home. After about three-and-a-half hours of pacing the floor, I turned on the TV, ready to instantly turn it off if the game was still on.

I heard, "The sweetest of all possible wins for ..." and I quickly clicked the TV off.

I figured at that moment Tech had won. A&M was the home team and ranked No. 5. Tech was unranked. I just couldn't imagine how the phrase "the sweetest of all possible wins" could apply to A&M.

When my wife got home and we started watching the tape, I didn't tell her what I knew. I just watched the game straight-faced and miserable. Tech led 17-16 in the last couple of minutes. The Aggies drove down the field and got into field-goal range with only a couple of seconds on the clock.

Then Tech coach Spike Dykes started using his remaining timeouts to try and ice the Aggies' kicker, Terry Venetoulias. I don't know that I've ever disliked a human being as much as I did Spike Dykes at that moment. I had to be mad at someone—especially after what I'd heard when I'd turned on the TV earlier.

Finally, Venetoulias kicked the ball from 21 yards outs. It wasn't blocked, so I figured it had to be wide. Wait, he made it! The Aggies had won 19-17 and remain undefeated (and would finish that magical season 12-1). I don't remember much about the next few minutes, but I do remember realizing at one point that I was kissing our dog. And I didn't care one bit.

JOHN BLACK, CLASS OF 1998, HOUSTON

A Memorable Meal

I'll never forget a special Saturday evening just before my 18th birthday. I grew up in Houston dreaming of being an Aggie—and also had decided I wanted to join the Fightin' Texas Aggie Band.

So on this wonderful evening in 1993, my father took me to see the A&M football team at Rice. We brought along a friend of my father's, Ben Bates, who had helped recruit me into the Aggie Band. After arriving shortly before kickoff, we were heading around the end zone to get to our seats when Ben saw a barbecue chicken stand.

There was an extraordinarily long line for this chicken, so Ben figured it must be worth the wait. Not wanting to miss any of the action, my dad and I found a good spot to watch on the terrace above the end zone seats.

The Owls took a 3-0 lead, and Ben had hardly moved in line. Then Rice kicked off to A&M freshman Leeland McElroy, and he exploded through the wedge and into the open field. The Aggie contingent roared with delight as McElroy sprinted 93 yards to give A&M the lead.

As my dad and I celebrated, we couldn't help but chuckle about Ben missing what was surely to be the highlight of the day. The line moved slowly but steadily for the chicken, just like the Rice offense. The Owls countered McElroy's run with a touchdown of their own to claim a three-point lead.

Meanwhile Ben had almost reached his goal of the apparently mouth-watering chicken. He was next in line when the Owls kicked off. My dad and I were standing in that prime spot to watch history unfold before us. As McElroy fielded the kickoff and broke through the wedge, I couldn't believe my eyes.

The freshman turned on the jets and left the Owls in his wake. Two consecutive kickoff returns for touchdowns to open the game!

As the Aggies kicked off, Ben strolled up and asked us what he'd missed.

My dad replied with a wink, "Only NCAA history. Hope you enjoy that chicken!"

NOAH WORLEY, CLASS OF 2002, McKINNEY

Tupac's Influence

What does the late rapper Tupac Shakur have to do with one of the most haunting losses in Aggie football history? Quite a bit, apparently, at least according to one A&M football player. Being a lifelong Aggie, this dark day in A&M football history that took place near the swamps in Lafayette, Louisiana, still cuts deep.

The memory of losing 29-22 to the Southwestern Louisiana Rajin' Cajuns in Lafayette on September 14, 1996, still haunts other Aggie fans, as well. But how many know the real reason we were upset that day—at least according to one former player.

On a February 2003 day, on a flight from Houston to Denver, I learned what he said was the truth about that day. It happened that a former A&M wide receiver, who would later play in the National Football League, was sitting next to me on the plane. We talked about Aggie football, and that loss came up.

He said that the players just didn't care that day. They were saddened and upset because Tupac, one of their favorite musicians, had died the day before. Shakur had been that target of an ambush style drive-by shooting after leaving the Mike Tyson–Bruce Sheldon boxing match in Las Vegas on September 7 and had lived for another six days in a Las Vegas hospital.

Shakur died on September 13, the day the Aggies traveled to Lafayette for one of their most stunning losses in the school's history.

CORY WALKER, CLASS OF 1998, AMARILLO

A Grand Day at Kyle

October 10, 1998, was a beautiful, sunny day for Texas A&M football. The Aggies were hosting the 1997 Big 12 champions, Nebraska, who'd whipped A&M the previous year in the Big 12 title game in San Antonio on its way to the national title.

As my friends and I walked from the apartment to Kyle Field, I just knew it was our day—A&M's day—to shine. Once we got to the stadium, I'd never heard it so loud before a game.

A&M pulled ahead quickly against the No. 2 Cornhuskers, thanks in part to an 81-yard touchdown pass to Chris Taylor and a 71-yard rumble by running back Ja'Mar Toombs to the Nebraska one-yard line. My friends and I yelled like never before—and everyone believed.

That belief got a bit of a scare, however, as Nebraska scored on our prevent defense in the second half and tightened the gap to 28-21. I let out a yell to "Remember the Alamodome!" and received a few chuckles back. Then cornerback Sedrick Curry intercepted a pass around midfield with 51 seconds remaining, and the Aggies held on for the victory.

The football team and the 12th Man would not be denied that day, when A&M beat its highest-ranked opponent to that point.

DANNY DAVIS, CLASS OF 1996, OAK HILL

Baseball and the Draft

On April 17, 1999, the No. 5 Aggies were playing No. 7 Baylor at Olsen Field in front of the largest paid crowd in A&M baseball history to that point. It was a great time to be an Aggie sports fan.

The Aggie hardballers were on their way to a second consecutive Big 12 championship, and the Aggie football team was just a few months removed from its classic Big 12 championship game win over Kansas State. This day would provide one of the rare occasions when the fans would be cheering for both sports at the same time—as it was also the first day of the NFL draft.

I remember thinking to myself how gorgeous the day had been, and the evening was turning out to be no different. Baylor drew first blood when it scored one run in the top of the first in what would prove to be a tight game to the finish. The Aggies answered with a run of their own in the bottom of the second.

It was becoming a game that under normal circumstances would have trumped any distraction. Then the public address announcements began.

"With the fifth pick in the third round, the Chicago Bears select offensive lineman from Texas A&M, Rex Tucker." Baseball "Whoops!" turned into football "Whoops!" for a minute. Before too long, the crowd heard, "With the seventh pick in the third round, the St. Louis Rams select defensive back from Texas A&M, Rich Coady." The former walk-on received a big "Whoop!" from the crowd.

Our focus was quickly redirected back to the game at hand when Baylor hit a two-run homer to go up 3-1 in the top of the fourth. The Aggies pulled within one with a home run of our own in the bottom of the fifth, but the Bears got it right back in the sixth by adding another run.

"With the 18th pick in the third round, the New York Giants select tight end from Texas A&M, Dan Campbell." Dan got a big "Whoop" and quite a few chuckles from our group as his speech about being proud to attend a school "where men like women and women like men...." from the 1998 Bonfire was still fresh on our minds.

The Aggies pulled back within one in the seventh, but it was getting down to nail-biting time. We were intensely focused on the game when *the* announcement was made. With every bit of showmanship and drama he could muster, the PA announcer began his last football related comment of the evening.

"With the 24th pick of the third round, the Dallas Cowboys..." a big "Whoop!" from the Olsen faithful followed that comment, not only for the Cowboys, but also in anticipation of who we *knew* it had to be—"...select linebacker from Texas A&M..." What had to have been the loudest non-baseball related roar ever at Olsen Field erupted into the night. "Dat Nguyen!"

The place went nuts—people were literally dancing in the aisles. Before we had a chance to settle down, the Aggies popped a two-run shot by Shawn Schumacher, a transfer from the Longhorns, out of the yard in the bottom of the eighth. It was the game-winner. It set off a raucous celebration that lasted into the night. It was a great night to be an Aggie, and a memory I'll never forget.

> "ANYTIME THE AGGIES PLAY, I'M GOING TO BE BETTING ON THEM."
>
> —A&M and NFL tight end Dan Campbell,
> at his final Aggie football banquet

JOHN "INDY" KORESSEL, CLASS OF 2000, EVANSVILLE, INDIANA, AND GALYN GAFFORD, CLASS OF 1999, AMARILLO

Baseball Aggie Alley Style

Our most memorable Aggie sports moments didn't occur in the fall at Kyle Field—but in the spring in what was Aggie Alley Baseball 1999 style. No more working through long weeks building Bonfire, and we didn't have to wait until Saturday for the big game.

We'd park our stadium-seating equipped "Blue Bomber" pickup in the rec center parking lot and fire up the barbecue pits. Occasionally we'd even feed the other teams' scrubs as they shagged balls during batting practice. Once the games started, we forgot all about A&M being a "football school."

We didn't always keep up with the score, but the players made sure we paid attention. Like the time "Ice Ice Baby" by Vanilla Ice had barely stopped blaring over Olsen's sound system when a home run by Sean Heaney dented the roof of our truck.

Sometimes it got pretty ugly out there in Aggie Alley, like the scuffle that ended with two guys rolling toward the outfield wall—right along with a keg. And we can't forget the buddy who went shoulder deep into a port-a-potty to recover some keys for a girl—ahh, true love.

Ray Dorr served as an inspiration not only to A&M's players but its football staff and fans.

We may have gained 20 pounds, drank too much, and destroyed our grades that semester. But we got our pictures taken on the back of a fire truck after a dumpster flamed up—no telling what happened there—and hung out with thousands at the Texas game that year, which turned Aggie Alley into the best party I've ever attended at A&M.

To top it all off, our Aggies gave us an unbelievable year, finishing 52-18 and earning a berth to the College World Series. We'll never forget Daylan Holt's 34 home runs that season or the homers off the bats of Steve Scarborough and Steven Truitt against Clemson in the stunning victory at Olsen that pushed us to the College World Series.

We can't imagine any A&M sports season ever matching Aggie Alley baseball in the spring of 1999.

ANONYMOUS

A Great Man

The disease came quickly. When I arrived for football camp in my job as a student equipment manager for Texas A&M in the summer of 1999, I asked one of my colleagues, "What's wrong with Coach Dorr?" Ray Dorr was then the genial and brilliant quarterbacks coach under R.C. Slocum.

He was still running around, playing the role of mad offensive scientist that was truly his life's calling, but there was a slight slur in his speech. The answer was sharp and direct: "He's got Lou Gehrig's disease."

The shock came slowly as I realized this was a terminal disease. As scrub student workers, most of the assistant coaches were somewhat friendly to us, and some were not. That's why, among our crew, Coach Dorr was admired and respected. He knew us all and never hesitated to speak to us and ask how things were going.

Over the 1999 football season, we watched as the disease slowly grasped Coach Dorr. His body became emaciated, his speech just a mumble, and he even had to wear a towel around his neck every day so that his deteriorating body wouldn't be a distraction to the players. He still coached those quarterbacks like no one else could, however.

Then came the news that Coach Dorr was going to retire immediately after the 1999 Alamo Bowl in San Antonio. Following A&M's 24-0 loss to Penn State in that game, we all were obviously frustrated. But there was Coach Dorr, managing a smile through all of the pain, slowly making his way around the locker room, hugging everyone.

Once a majority of the players had said goodbye, I made my way over to him and gave him a hug. He smiled and said, "Thanks." I wiped away a few tears and got back to work—and that was the last I ever saw of a great man.

Coach Dorr died in March 2001 of Lou Gehrig's disease.

An offensive genius, father figure to some and respected by all, coach Ray Dorr was one of a kind.

BOB PALMAREZ, CLASS OF 1973, KARNES CITY

The Amazing Day

By far one of the most memorable moments in my Texas A&M life was the first football game at Kyle Field following the tragedy of September 11, 2001, when terrorists struck America.

The events of September 11 inspired some A&M students to organize a movement to tell everyone attending the September 22, 2001, game at Kyle Field to wear red, white, and blue to correspond with the third, second, and first decks. They also printed up 70,000 shirts that said, "Standing for America" to raise money for the 9-11 relief effort.

The impact of the red, white, and blue decks was inspiring, and I still get teary-eyed thinking about it. Honestly, it made me grateful to be an Aggie, because no other university could have done what we did that day. Our message was simple: We are the Aggie family, fiercely loyal to each other and the country in which we live.